THE BOOK OF
WITCHY
WELLBEING

THE BOOK OF
WITCHY
WELLBEING

RITUALS, RECIPES, AND SPELLS FOR SACRED SELF-CARE

CERRIDWEN GREENLEAF

CICO BOOKS
LONDON NEW YORK

May we all find healing and love along our path to a life of peace. xo

Published in 2021 by CICO Books
An imprint of Ryland Peters & Small Ltd
20–21 Jockey's Fields   341 E 116th St
London WC1R 4BW   New York, NY 10029

www.rylandpeters.com

10 9 8 7 6 5 4 3 2 1

A CIP catalog record for this book is available
from the Library of Congress and the British
Library.

ISBN: 978-1-80065-032-9

Printed in China

Designer: Geoff Borin
Illustrator: Emma Garner (artwork on
page 14 by Amy Louise Evans)
Commissioning editor: Kristine Pidkameny
Senior editor: Carmel Edmonds
Senior designer: Emily Breen
Art director: Sally Powell
Head of production: Patricia Harrington
Publishing manager: Penny Craig
Publisher: Cindy Richards

SAFETY NOTE: Please note that while the
use of essential oils, herbs, incense, and
particular practices refer to healing benefits,
they are not intended to replace diagnosis of
illness or ailments, or healing or medicine.
Always consult your doctor or other health
professional in the case of illness, pregnancy,
and personal sensitivities and conditions.
Test any homemade beauty products on your
wrist before using to check for any irritation.
Neither the author nor the publisher can be
held responsible for any claim arising out
of the general information, recipes, and
practices provided in this book.

CONTENTS

INTRODUCTION: THE ART OF SACRED SELF-CARE

When you awaken each morning, what comes first into your mind? Ideally, it should be a sense of the possible and of your very aliveness. And, indeed, every day is alive with possibility. Every single day is a good day to exist on this abundant planet that gives everything we need: air, water, heat, and earth and all the good things that come from them. These elements make up the building blocks for life and also connect us to the sacred in nature. Holding an awareness of this origin will keep you conscious of yourself, your breath, your energy levels, and how you feel in your body. As you wake up every day, you should connect to your body and breathe each new day in. If you are an early riser, all the better, as the dew in the dawn is extremely good for you. I learned this from my friend's Chinese grandmother, Su, who lived to 108 and attributed this to doing a bit of tai chi every morning in the backyard (though I know she also drank many pots of herbal tea).

What I suggest you do is find the daily rituals that are soothing to you in body, mind, and soul. Like the wise elder Su, you should breathe, move, and awaken into your day with awareness and mindfulness. Meditations, prayers, and practices can make you feel grounded and whole, but it won't happen overnight, and can and should take time. What really nurtures you? What really quiets your mind and fills you with peace and positivity?

In this book, I suggest rituals that will enable you to up your wellness quotient by harnessing the power of flowers, herbs, crystals, candles, and more. You can also grow your craft with the natural magic that stems from our Earth, the four elements, and the energy of the moon, stars, and planets. Learn how you can cleanse your home and create a peace-filled, serene space for you and your loved ones with incense, essential oils, and simple spells. Discover how you can restore both your sense of self and vigor with herbal preparations, as well as meditations and prayers for the equally important care of your soul. Create your own Book of Shadows, a personal record of all your spells and recipes, and journal in it about your progress with these approaches to sacred care as you listen deeply to your heart and discover what feeds you.

My intention is to offer a wellness retreat for you in book form. The recipes, rituals, and practices herein have soothed my soul, fed my spirit, calmed my mind, and gladdened my heart. I have shared them with friends, clients, and loved ones as we have amped up our approaches to self-care over the last decade. Witches are often well ahead of the pack in terms of the healing arts, and every spellcaster I know has been busily endeavoring to expand their repertoire of rites and enchantments, as well as teas, tinctures, and pagan prescriptions, for total wellbeing. While my parents still wonder why I majored in medieval studies in university, I continue to be grateful about that choice as I am able to research and revive some of the best of the old ways that our foremothers used centuries ago. Brews from nearly forgotten plants that have fallen out of fashion two millennia ago can be a balm for our modern maladies. Essential oils and potions that remain in use from ancient Egypt and Greece are more indispensable than ever before. All this wisdom passed down from hedgewitch healers can add more joy to your days. Slow down a bit, breathe, and ground yourself in nature—witchy wellbeing is the most practical magic of all!

Chapter 1

HAPPY, HEALTHY YOU:
Enchanted Ideas and Mindfulness Magic

We are living in a time when wellness is a topic on nearly everyone's mind, and this will only increase as health has become even more of a focus for so many of us. Cooking nutritious meals, meditation, and long luxurious walks in parks and around our neighborhoods have become healthy new habits embraced by many. Friends of mine that you could once barely pry from their offices have been suddenly rhapsodizing about the newfound pleasure of gardening and cooking fresh, homegrown veggies. I have noted all this approvingly as it indicates a newfound connection to our earth, which is the very core of wellbeing. Our Mother Earth heals us—in turn, we should do the same. Wicca is a spiritual practice that is centered in earth wisdom. Right now, spells for healing are the most important magic we can do.

SET YOUR HEALTH INTENTION

To embark upon lifelong wellbeing, you will need to bring awareness to every day of your life. A regular ritual for your health can in time become a daily intention.

Adorn one of your favorite home spaces with fresh flowers and candles in colors that represent healing: yellow, red, and green. Every morning for seven days, light the candles and contemplate your future self in an optimal state of health, while you repeat this spell:

Today I arise on this glorious day

Under this rising sun, hear me say:

I will walk in wellness in every way

For body, mind, and soul, I pray.

Blessed be, and may it be so.

CLARIFYING YOUR HEALING INTENTION

Think about what you need before you craft any of the spells in this chapter (or indeed this book). Your reason is your intention, and is the focus of your ritual; holding this in mind will direct your personal energy. One basic guideline is that the creation of ritual should be not only for you and your loved ones, but also "for the greater good." Some examples of reasons include:

- To bring renewed health to body and spirit

- To bless a personal space or family home

- To bless and bring calm and contentment to the people in your life

- To bring about a more peaceful community and world

UNLEASH YOUR VISIONARY POWERS

Mugwort has long been used in magical workings, starting in Mesopotamia and expanding throughout Europe, Asia, and now the world. It is used by seers and shamans for achieving new levels of consciousness. Mugwort is especially good for the mental plane and helps overcome headaches and soothes anxiety for mental balance and calm (see page 78). This spell can sharpen your sixth sense, which will guide you and enhance every aspect of your life.

Light the candle, and then light the stick of vanilla incense and place it in a fire-safe burner. Place the yellow flower and vase to one side of the incense burner. On the other side, place a bowl containing a citrine crystal. Yellow symbolizes intelligence and mental clarity.

In your teakettle, boil the water. Pour it into the bowl, add the teaspoon of mugwort, and stir. Once it has cooled completely, dip your fingers in the water and touch your "third eye" at the center of your forehead. Now speak aloud:

Diana, Goddess of the Moon,

Fill me with your presence divine.

I seek your vision; lend me this boon.

Greatest seer, may the second sight be mine.

And so it is. And may it be soon.

After a few moments of contemplation, extinguish the candle. Your new psychic abilities will become apparent soon.

Gather together

Yellow candle

Stick of vanilla incense

Incense burner

Single yellow flower in a vase

Bowl

Citrine crystal

1 teaspoon dried mugwort

ELEMENTAL MAGIC

You are now embarking on spellwork to create important changes in your life and to become more connected to the world around you. Wicca is, after all, an Earth path, so working in harmony with the elements of which the earth is made is an important step in your personal practice. Just as there are specific influences in the stars and planets astrologically, rhythmic phases of the moon, and a range of crystalline color powers in stones, there are very particular powers in the elements you can call on in your ritual work.

Water, fire, earth, and air are the four elements of the ancients and were developed during the time of the original pagans. The ancient philosopher Empedocles of Sicily refined the theory of Earth elements between 420 and 410 BCE and, despite our many modern beliefs, we still hold with the basics of early metaphysics, where science and spirit conjoin.

Water

Water is the fluid state of matter, the nurturer of all life, and essential for all continued existence. The blood that flows through the veins of animals is mostly water, with trace minerals flowing within it. Water cleanses, nourishes crops, and washes away what no longer serves a purpose. Water is the opposite of earth in that it flows: it lacks stability. Even ice, water in a stable form, can melt. Water in our rivers, lakes, and oceans is ever-changing. Water is a very important cleansing and blessing element to bring into play in your ritual. A fountain or bowl of water in your home represents the all-important water of life. You can use water for any kind of releasing ritual. Water signs Cancer, Scorpio, and Pisces should perform water rituals to stay in tune with their sensitive, creative natures.

Water blessing rite

Part of living in balance is remaining in contact with all elements. If we are too involved in one element, we will feel an unease. For example, if someone smokes tobacco or other substances a lot, he or she will be filled with too much fire energy and can even "dry out." This is easily remedied by balancing out with the opposite of fire, water. This beautifully simple water rite will restore your spirit.

Find a nearby body of water, such as the ocean, a river or lake, or even your own bathtub, and bring a small bottle of water from home with you. Stand as near as you are able to the body of water and quiet your mind. Kneel and speak aloud:

We all come from the Goddess

And to her we shall return;

Like a drop of water,

Flowing to the ocean.

Pour some of the water you brought with you into your hand and put it on your face and repeat the chant. Pour the rest of the water into the body of water and repeat the song. You will now be rejuvenated and rebalanced.

Earth

Earth is the manifestation of the solid. It is real and tangible matter. The Earth gives us intransigence, constancy, and durability. All beings on this beautiful planet are made of earth, and we are part of a natural, magical system. Earth is a stable material and element. To embody its presence on your altar (see page 26), you can grow a flowering plant or you can place some sand in a shell to represent this element. And at the end of our lives, we once again return to the Earth. You should call on the element of earth when you want to become more grounded or to manifest something new and tangible into your life.

Earth signs Taurus, Virgo, and Capricorn should perform earth rituals on a regular basis to stay centered. Earth signs are always thought of as the most stable, practical, and organized of all the signs, but there is the other side of the coin that often manifests in those drawn to Dark Moon magic: the sensual, quiet type who works and prefers to entertain at home and has the enviable lair. Tried and true earth rituals include walking meditations, circling in a sacred grove, and a guided visualization of entering into ancient Mesopotamian goddess Inanna's cave. Some magical earth deities to work with are the Green Man, Venus of Willendorf, Persephone, and elves or trolls.

Earthing: an element ritual

I love that earthing is coming into vogue as more and more people realize the need to spend time with nature. Earthing is the practice of tapping into earth energy directly by walking barefoot and collecting the beneficial electrons naturally generated by the soil beneath your feet. It is a ritual for reconnecting with the Earth in order to feel more grounded. You don't need to go to a mountain top to get in touch with Mother Earth—try your own backyard or a nearby park, or visit a friend's farm.

Whichever you choose, make sure it is a dry, sunny, and warm day. Just take yourself and a blanket. Find a place that looks right to you and that you are drawn to and set your blanket and any belongings down so you are holding nothing. Remove your shoes and socks and stand on the earth itself. Wiggle your toes and really feel the soil underneath you. As you stand, speak the following prayer aloud:

Mother, I call upon you to support me

And I promise in turn, I will support you.

I am grounded in you and with you.

My love for you is as big as the world.

Blessed be thee

For eternity.

Now spend as much time as you like in your sacred earthing space. Commune with nature safely in the embrace of Mother Earth.

Air

Air is the unseen form of matter and is formless, but is ever-changing, possessing mobility and dynamism. The oxygen in the very air we breathe is essential to the continuation of all life on Earth. Wind creates movement and effects change. Air signs Gemini, Libra, and Aquarius are known for their brilliance and superior communication skills. They can maintain these skills with rituals invoking the element of air, such as singing, chanting, and conscious breathing.

Air element rite

Sometimes we all require help understanding what we need for ourselves. If you are seeking additional insight on how to better serve your own needs or even to identify what they are, ask the messenger god Mercury to come to your aid. Mercury prevails over communication, speed, mental clarity, and fun. All things yellow and citrus can bring forth Mercury's bright presence. Try this invocation to make contact.

Gather together

3 yellow candles

Neroli essential oil

Bergamot essential oil

Paper and pen

On a Wednesday evening (Wednesday is ruled by Mercury), anoint yourself and the candles with bergamot and neroli oil. Light the candles and meditate on the flames, breathing deeply and filling your lungs with the fiery citrus scent. Holding both hands out, palms up, say:

Messenger of the gods,

Bring me your news.

Tonight, in this fire and flame,

I call upon you this day by your name.

Mercury, messenger and god,

I will listen for your word on the wing.

Blessed be, to thee and me.

Extinguish the candles. Now go to sleep with your dream journal nearby and see what messages appear in your dreams. Alternatively, close your eyes and take up your pen for "automatic writing," allowing your hand and wrist to relax until you see what words take shape on the page. Heed the missive, as it has come to you from Mercury himself.

Fire

Fire is heat and is the most visible form of energy. Fire is a powerful element, as it can transform and change the other elements. If you watch the flicker of your candle flame, the embers of your incense, or the blaze of your fireplace, you will see a constant transmutation of matter. Fire has the ability to both excite and incite us, and fire is necessary to bring about change. Fire signs Aries, Leo, and Sagittarius are known for their strength and vibrancy. They can maintain this by invoking their personal element. A simple, powerful, and direct way you can do this is through candle magic.

Self-healing fire rite

This fire element ritual might become something you perform regularly, as it is fortifying to your spirit and feels simply wonderful.

Take the pillar candle and anoint it with bergamot essential oil. Place the orange, which represents vibrant health, beside the candle. Scratch your own name into the candle and write: "I love [your name]." Light the candle and say four times:

I love me. I love _____ [your name].

Extinguish the candle when you have finished.

Repeat this ritual of charging the candle with love toward yourself every night before bed and every morning when you arise. Your mood and sense of self will grow in positivity.

Gather together

Large red pillar candle

Bergamot essential oil

Orange

ENCOURAGEMENT SPELL: QUELL NEGATIVE SELF-TALK

As the sun sets on a waning moon day, you can quiet the inner voices of negativity and inner criticism that get in the way of simple joy. When our moon ebbs, another grows forth, and so it goes for our creativity cycles.

Gather together

1 teaspoon patchouli resin

1 teaspoon rose hips

Vanilla bean

Charcoal wafer

Fireproof dish or incense burner

Incense bowl

Gray candle

Grind together the patchouli resin, rose hips, and the whole vanilla bean. Burn this mixture on the charcoal in the incense bowl on your altar (see page 26). Light a gray candle (for protection) and meditate on the flame. As you meditate, think about whether you sometimes doubt yourself and your instincts. Visualize clearing that from your mind. Think about your talents and your potential as you chant:

La lune, Goddess of the Moon,

As you may grow, so do I.

Here, tonight, under your darkest light,

I shall embrace all within me that is good and right,

And bid goodbye to all the rest. Blessed be.

Blow out the candle and cast it into a fireplace, an outdoor firepot, or wherever it can be melted down completely and safely. You must completely destroy the candle, as it contains the energy of your inner critic. You should feel lighter and brighter almost immediately!

SHANDANA SPELL

Sandalwood, from the Sanskrit word *chandana*, has been used for thousands of years in India. The woody, sweet smell clears your mind and reconnects you to the earth.

Gather together

Brown candle

1 tablespoon (15 ml) sandalwood essential oil

¼ cup (60 ml) almond base oil

2 drops lemon essential oil

2 drops amber essential oil

Double-boiler pan

Ceramic bowl

Anoint the candle with some of the sandalwood oil. Carefully warm the rest of the sandalwood oil with the other oils in a double-boiler, then transfer into the bowl and let cool for a few moments. When warm to the touch, dip your left ring finger into the oil and anoint your "third eye," located just above the eyes in the center of your forehead. Sitting in the cross-legged lotus position, whisper three times:

Come to me clarity, come to me peace,

Come to me wisdom, come to me bliss.

Meditate for twenty minutes, and then massage the warmed oil into your feet. You will be utterly blissfully grounded now.

CALMING CURE TO HEAL FROM HURT

To help heal yourself from a major upset in life, try this soothing potion.

Gather together

¼ cup (60 ml) jojoba or almond base oil

Small dark-colored sealable bottle

4 drops rose essential oil

4 drops vanilla essential oil

4 drops clove essential oil

4 tiny rose quartz crystals

Handkerchief or cotton ball

Pour the base oil into the bottle and add the essential oils. Seal the bottle and then gently shake it to mix. Now add the rose quartz crystals into the vial. Pour a few drops of the mixture onto the handkerchief or cotton ball and dab it lightly on your temples, neck, and shoulders, gently rubbing in a circular motion. Silently call upon Venus to assist you. Keep the calming oil to use any time you need tranquility; it should last at least six months if kept in a cool, dry cupboard.

PEACE, LOVE, AND HEALING RITUAL

The ultimate alchemy is to generate positive energy that spirals outward, improving everything in its path. I know of shamans and wise women who have dedicated their lives to doing good works, including some crones who practice in the ancient rainforest to protect the trees, and aborigines who spend their "dreamtime" repairing the earth. Join their efforts with this healing ritual.

Place the rose in the vase or bowl of water. Alongside, lay the garlic clove, which represents healing, and some rose incense. Light the incense, then take a bundle of white sage, light it, and pass the smoke over your altar to "smudge" the space. Chant:

War and grief will come to an end,

We walk the path of peace,

Love thy neighbor as thy self,

All we need is love.

With harm to none, only understanding.

You can also contribute to universal peace and healing by burning a white candle, anointed with rose oil, during a waning moon on Saturday, Saturn's Day.

Gather together

White rose

Vase or bowl of freshly drawn water

Garlic clove

Rose incense

White sage

ENERGY SHIELD POTPOURRI

This will safeguard you and your loved ones from psychic vampires—people who drain your mental and emotional energy—and from outside influences that could be negative or disruptive. Brew up a batch whenever you feel the need to infuse your home and heart with the energies of protection.

Gather together

¼ cup (10 g) dried sage leaves

¼ cup (10 g) dried rosemary

4 dried bay laurel leaves

1 tablespoon dried basil

1 teaspoon dried dill weed

1 drop garlic oil

1 tablespoon dried juniper berries

Saucepan filled with water

Mix the herbs, oil, and berries together by hand. While you are doing this, close your eyes and visualize yourself and your space protected by a boundary of glowing white light. Imagine that the light runs through you to the herbs in your hand and charges them with the energy of safety, sanctity, and protection. Add the mixture to a pan filled with simmering water. When the aromatic mist and steam start to rise, intone aloud:

By my own craft, I have made this brew;

Peace and joy reigns over this home anew.

By my own will, I make this charm;

This potion protects all from harm.

With harm to none and health to all, blessed be!

MINDFUL WALKING MEDITATION

Moving every day is a way to commit to your aliveness and wellness. The ancients had a concept of moving prayer, which was to either walk through holy temples or visualize moving through them in your mind, as a form of prayer which was very effective for connecting to spirit. When medieval cathedrals were built, they often had a labyrinth for this purpose. The labyrinth represented wholeness to the ancients, combining the circle and the spiral in one archetypal image. The labyrinth is unicursal, meaning there is only one path, both in and out. Put simply, it represents a journey into the self, into your own center, and back into the world again. As a prayer and meditation tool, labyrinths are peerless; they awaken intuition.

As did our forebears, you can carry out this meditation either in your mind, using your imagination, or walking.

Do your best to relax before you begin. Deep breaths will help a great deal. If you have a specific question in mind, think it or whisper it to yourself. If you are in an actual labyrinth and meet others on the pilgrim's path as you are walking, simply step aside and let them continue on their journey as you do the same. The three stages of the labyrinth walk are as follows:

Purgation: Here is where you free your mind of all worldly concerns. It is a release, a letting go. Still your mind and open your heart. Shed worries and emotion as you step out on the path.

Illumination: When you have come to the center, you are in the place of illumination. Here, you should stay as long as you feel the need to pray and meditate. In this quiet center, the heart of the labyrinth, you will receive messages from the Divine or from your own higher power. Illumination can also come from deep inside yourself.

Union: This last phase is where you will experience union with the divine—you will know when you have reached it. In *Walking a Sacred Path*, historian and spiritual teacher Lauren Artress says that as you "walk the labyrinth, you become more empowered to find and do the work you feel your soul requires."

Use the rituals in this chapter to become one with yourself and find peace within. May you use this learned tranquility to better participate in other rituals that focus on important aspects of your life.

Chapter 2

CREATING AN ALTAR:
Your Personal Renewal Center

To a large extent, a dedication to your personal wellbeing involves energy management—your own energy and that which is demanded from you by the world and by your interactions and relationships with others. Establishing a sacred space in your home—an altar—as a personal sanctuary is essential. This holistic approach provides the opportunity for deep inner work, since within your sacred space you can experience meaningful exploration to transform your life.

YOUR TRUE NORTH: AN ALTAR DEDICATED TO WELLNESS

Your altar is your sacred workspace, a place imbued with your personal pagan power. This will become one of the most sacred spaces in your home and will doubtless become a touchstone for you where you immediately step into the realm of magic.

Gather together

Table, at least 2 x 2 feet (60 x 60 cm)

Pure white sheet of fabric, large enough to drape over the table touching the floor

2 candles in matching holders

Incense burner

Whatever you use for your altar (perhaps you have a favorite antique table, at once simple and ornate), it will represent the four directions of the compass. I recommend setting up the altar to face north, long believed to be the origin of primordial energy. North is the direction of midnight, and an altar oriented in this fashion promises potent magic. Drape the white fabric over your table, then take the candles and place them in the two farthest corners. Place the incense burner exactly in the middle.

Setting up your healing altar

Your altar is key to your magical workings, so it needs to be infused with YOU. Here is where you can fully apply your personal design and creativity. Tap into your intuition and let it be your guide in this sacred shrine. Select objects that appeal to you symbolically to place on your altar.

Crystals may include rose quartz, amethyst, quartz crystal, or turquoise, or any other minerals that promote healing and add supportive energy during your process. I have a candlestick of purest amethyst crystal, my birthstone. When I gaze on the candle flame refracted through the beautiful purple gemstone, I feel the fire within me.

Fill the incense burner. If you don't have a favorite incense yet, start with the ancient essence of frankincense.

Focus on what you wish to heal. You may wish to write out an intention list of your desires. While you hold your healing intention

in your mind, begin to notice what would support your intention. It may be a picture of a healed person, a symbol, or a picture of a spiritual master, such as St. Francis, the Blessed Mother, Kuan Yin, or the Buddha. Choose whomever you feel most connected with.

Honor Mother Earth by placing a bowl of water on the altar, as well as an additional white candle to banish bad energy. Add items to represent the elements of fire (see page 17) and earth (see page 14). You can also add fresh flowers and pictures or a sculpture of your animal allies and totems (see page 133).

You should decorate your altar until it is utterly and completely pleasing to your eye. The ritual of creating an altar provides support to your process, and inculcates your altar with the magic that lives inside you, that lives inside all of us, and magnifies the ceremonial strength of your workspace. After you've been working spells for a while, an energy field will radiate from your altar; it will become your true north.

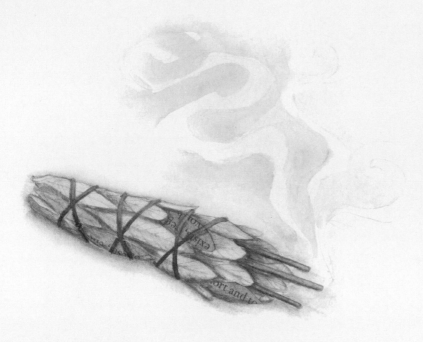

Imbuing your sacred space with your personal energy

Once you have created your altar, you must make it sacred to prepare both it and you for rituals and casting spells. Make it a space where you can listen to yourself, which leads to a deeper inner wisdom.

You might use a smudge stick made of sage, evergreen, or cedar to prepare yourself and your space. Light the stick and allow the smoke to pass over the altar to clear away earthly demands and confusion.

Some people choose to use holy water or wear a gold cross as they work through their healing process, while others place a glass bowl of blessed saltwater on their altar to keep the space clear of negative energy.

You may wish to play classical or soothing music in the background while you work, but I prefer the sound of my drum and rattles.

Once you have created your space, remove all distractions (turn off your phone), and sit quietly in a comfortable position. I suggest that you sit rather than lie down because you will be less likely to fall asleep. Now close your eyes and take a few deep breaths to quiet yourself. Sit by your altar for an hour or so as you are inculcated with healing. Open your eyes, arise, and offer a silent thank you for the blessing of your wellbeing.

SUPER-NATURAL SHRINES

Using your sacred spaces often really does imbue them with your personal energy and makes them more of a power center for you so your magic grows. I suggest you dress your altar for seasonal and high holidays, such as sabbats (see pages 30–31), with beloved objects, candles, flowers, deity statues, and crystals.

Finding inspiration

As I write this, the Winter Solstice approaches so I will adorn my sacred space with a white birch branch with delicate lichen barely clinging to the bark and search for other gifts from nature that represent this time of year. What speaks to you? Think of how a frozen lake glistens with many colors and the mystery that lies beneath the surface, both of which can be represented by an iridescent and glittery chunk of labradorite crystal for your altar. As you take a walk in the darkening days in the countdown to the Winter Solstice, you might collect a fallen leaf, which is a perfect dried emblem of the changing of the season, or one tiny acorn, tucked in the roots of an old oak tree, which you can place on your altar as a symbol of all potentiality.

If you pass by a yard sale, you may spy something beautiful, such as a piece of ornately carved ivory, an antique whale-tooth scrimshaw depicting an Inuit ritual, and you would instantly know it was perfect for your sacred space. Why not also try your hand at art? Paint on your altar a triptych—the hoary sky, palest sun struggling to shine, a low-hung harvest moon, all beautiful blues with a sapphire night sky and silver stars.

Thinking about the heavens above and the firmament in which hang the stars, moon, sun, and all the planets, you might be struck by a sense of the sacred. It is so special to be alive on this planet; maybe an accident and most definitely a miracle. As you think about it, perhaps you can almost feel the swing of Earth on its axis as it spins around the sun, and now more than ever, feel so very alive.

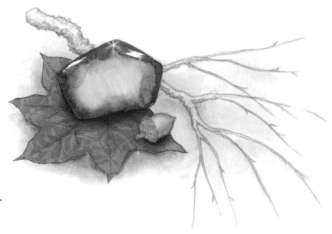

Seasonal altar suggestions

Mark your witchy calendar with these sabbats as they will become anchoring events in your year—and life.

The four major sabbats

Candlemas (also known as Imbolc)

Date: February 2

Colors: White, light blue, and light green.

Altar offerings: Sprouting seeds, a goblet of cider, and first blossoms, such as snowdrops, crocuses, violets, and irises.

Intention: As the season begins to shift from winter, so will I open to inner change.

Beltane

Date: May 1

Colors: Grass green and pink.

Altar offerings: Spring leaves, a bowl of newly fallen rain, brightly colored ribbons, small herbs, and mayflowers.

Intention: I celebrate the warmth of spring and the fire of love in my life.

Lammas

Date: August 1

Colors: Bright green and gold.

Altar offerings: Berries, vegetables from the garden, leaves, brightly colored flowers in full bloom, and a loaf of bread.

Intention: As harvest season begins, I am grateful for and will share this bounty of blessings.

Samhain

Date: October 31

Colors: Purple, deep red, brown, and deep orange.

Altar offerings: Carved pumpkins, orange leaves, sweet pumpkin or chocolate spirit cakes, and a goblet of red wine.

Intention: As the veil between worlds disappears this day, I call upon the elders, ancestors, and loved ones who have crossed over for wisdom.

The four lesser sabbats

Vernal Equinox (also known as Ostara)

Date: March 21

Colors: Light green and light yellow.

Altar offerings: Seedlings, budding and sprouting branches, a bowl of flower bulbs, and eggs.

Intention: On this day when light is in balance, I fully embrace sacred self-care for balance and in my life and work.

Summer Solstice (also known as Litha)

Date: June 21

Colors: Bright yellow.

Altar offerings: Freshly foraged weeds and herbs, veggies, leaves, and fruit.

Intention: On this midsummer day with the sun's full power, I own my full personal power to bring dreams into fruition.

Winter Solstice (also known as Yule)

Date: December 21

Colors: White, light blue, silver, and black.

Altar offerings: A bowl of snow, winter photos, seeds, and icicle-shaped clear crystals.

Intention: I intend to spend this shortest day in community with friends, family, and fellow pagans to share our stories and strengthen connections.

Autumnal Equinox (also known as Mabon)

Date: September 21

Colors: Gold, brown, and orange.

Altar offerings: Squash and pumpkins, bounty from the garden, acorns and other nuts, colored leaves, corn, and fall flowers.

Intention: As summer shifts to fall, I will let go of anything which no longer serves me.

FLOWERS OF FORTUNE ALTAR ENCHANTMENT

The more you tend your altar, the more of your personal magic is inculcated in that sacred space. In regard to the great magical undertaking of your own wellbeing, it is vital that you imbue your altar with your essence and your energy. For this enchantment, start at noon on a Sunday.

Gather together

Photo of you

Favorite piece of birthstone jewelry

Small pedestal

Vase filled with fresh water

4 flowers, any of the following: yellow daisy, yellow rose, sunflower, or a yellow lily

Select the photo of yourself: it should be one that you love where you look both healthful and joyful. Place it on a pedestal on your altar along with the piece of jewelry. In front of the pedestal, place a small vase with your four Flowers of Fortune. These posies will bring you abundance, which includes both wealth and health. The yellow signifies the vigor and sun-blessed energy that will increase your strength and vivacity every time you speak the following spell:

On this earth and under these stars, I call upon the Gods to bring great help and good fortune to me, _____ [your name].

[At this point, put on the beloved piece of jewelry and wear it as you continue the spell.]

In this air and through these waters, speed fortune here in my name of _____ [your name].

[Now touch the stone in the ring.]

Through the fire and through the rain, bring me gladness, goodwill, and great health!

Bring them to me, here and now.

Remove the jewelry and place it back on your altar. Repeat the spell the next day at noon for a week. Each day, you should awaken feeling cheerier and more content.

LUNAR ALTARATIONS

I often switch up my altar adornments every two or three days with the changing of the lunar cycles. Here are some suggestions for altar combinations and activities to help you shift your personal energy in accordance with the moon phases.

• New Moon Mini Altar: orange candles, yellow jade, neroli essential oil, and cinnamon incense for joy, success, strength, and creativity. Write and speak goals. As we all know, the dark moon is the new moon and the optimal time for new beginnings and it is an excellent time for you to undertake a new pledge to personal wellness. This is the time to let go of old ways and take up new directions.

• Waxing Moon Mini Altar: Green candle, peridot, clary sage essential oil, and jasmine incense for prosperity, expansion, and healing. Speak your new hopes.

• Half Moon Mini Altar: Brown candles, tiger eye, and amber oil and incense for grounding and stability. Hold your focus and feel your rootedness to Earth.

• Waxing Gibbous Moon Altar: Red candles, garnet, and rose essential oil and incense for this time to enjoy your life, relax, and let go. Simply be, let things flow, and spend time with friends, family, and your loved one.

• Full Moon Mini Altar: Blue candles, amethyst, bergamot essential oil, and sandalwood incense for this phase of maximum healing and transformation. Meditate upon and feel your full power. This is the time when the sun and moon face each other directly and there is much potential for real illumination. Seeds planted in the new moon will now come into fruition.

CANDLE MAGIC SIGIL SPELL

Carving symbols onto your candles is a simple and profound way to deepen your magic. What symbols are meaningful to you? Certain crosses, vines, flowers, hieroglyphs, and many other images have deep magical associations, so you should feel free to delve in and experiment to find the symbols that work best for you in your spells.

If you are like me and have the artistic skill of a toddler, you can simply carve hearts, suns, and stars into the sides of pillar candles. I just did exactly that as I was feeling a bit low because of the negative daily news. I took a bright yellow pillar candle and carved a sun into the side, placed it on my altar, lit the candle, and intoned:

Sol, our star,

Bring your light

Which none can mar.

Burn long and bright

Keep bad news afar.

Send negativity out of sight.

So mote it be.

I meditated on the candle flame and envisioned sunnier days. Find your special symbols and sigils and use them often and they will grow in power for your personal use.

WHAT ARE SIGILS?

The term sigil derives from the word "seal." A sigil is a magical glyph or symbol that is used in ritual to deepen your focus or intensify magical powers. Methods for devising sigils for spellwork include using the planetary glyphs of astrology, runes, Enochian tablets, letters, numbers, or even mystical cyphers, such as hermetic crosses or kabbalistic signs.

BLISSINGS BOX: HERBS FOR SELF-LOVE

Scent is such a powerful signal to the brain. Altars are perfect places to keep treasure boxes of ceremonial incenses and other sacred tools. In the following ritual, herbs and flowers remind you to hold yourself in the highest esteem, and every time you need a lift, you can open this box of bliss and breathe in pure love. Try to perform this rite during a new moon.

Gather together

¼ cup (5 g) pink rose petals

¼ cup (10 g) dried lavender

¼ cup (10 g) dried oregano

Small mixing bowl

3 drops lavender essential oil

3 drops rose essential oil

Small wooden box with lid

Pink jade, red jade, or rose quartz crystal

Place the flower petals and herbs into the bowl and gently mix together. Add the essential oils and mix again, then fill the box with the herbal mix. Settle the crystal in the herbs right at the top, then close the lid and place the box on your altar. Each night, open the box up and breathe in the lovely fragrance that will envelope you in an aura of love.

EFFORTLESS ENCHANTMENT: EASY DIY INSPIRATION INCENSE

An essential tool for regular use in your altar is incense, along with a firesafe burner. I am always looking for new incense recipes that are really quick and easy to do. Sometimes, we need big magic in a short amount of time. The following approach to homemade incense is marvelous for its simplicity, arresting aromas, and rapid results.

Gather together

1 tablespoon dried rose petals

1 tablespoon dried lavender

Mortar and pestle

2 drops sandalwood essential oil

Cinnamon stick

Small glass jar with lid

Charcoal wafer

Fireproof dish or incense burner

Matches

Place the rose petals and lavender into the mortar and grind together using the pestle until broken down into small pieces and well mixed. Add the sandalwood essential oil. Break the cinnamon stick into small pieces, then add to the herb mixture and grind lightly with the pestle until all is thoroughly mixed. This is your incense mix that can be stored in the jar.

To use, place one of the charcoal wafers into the fireproof dish. Carefully put a heaping teaspoon of the incense onto the wafer and light it with a match. Anytime you are in need of a lift or wisdom from above, this incense will inspire and elevate your spirit as it pleases your senses.

SACRED SMOKE SPELL

Every time I light incense, I carry the awareness that it is a holy act. I also hold the intention that this is a simple yet mighty magic that will infuse my home almost instantaneously with sacred energy. Your altar is your personal power center and burning incense there inculcates and deepens the magic in this space.

Place the god or goddess in the front center of your altar and set the dish filled with incense in front of the deity. Speak this prayer spell as you light this incense on your altar:

As beloved ancestors and gods great and good do aim,

I light this incense in your honor and in your name.

As this herb burns, energies move and dance in flame.

As this smoke rises, blessings grow and these I claim.

All gratitude to you, _____ [fill in with the name of the deity]

So mote it be.

Gather together

Statue or image of a deity that has special meaning to you

Incense of your choice

Fireproof dish or incense burner

WAFTING WELLNESS: INCENSES FOR RELAXATION AND RESTORATION

These gentle floral and herbal incenses can aid you to achieving a meditative and contemplative state of mind. Burn any one of them as a stick or cone and you'll hone your "om."

- Lavender • Sandalwood • Jasmine • Rose
- Vanilla • Cedar • Lemongrass

CLEARING AND CLEANSING INCENSE

Energetic cleansing on a regular basis is vital for wellbeing. The energy of other people can settle around you as a kind of metaphysical clutter, so I suggest regular clearing. I do mine every Saturday afternoon and go into every room of the house, doubling up the amount of cleansing incense used in any shrine and altar spaces as well as at the front and back door.

Gather together

2 teaspoons finely chopped dried lemon peel

2 tablespoons dried rosemary

Fireproof dish or incense burner

Matches

To create the incense, layer the rosemary leaf on the bottom of a fireproof dish. The rosemary burns so well you don't need a charcoal as the natural oils in the leaves cause a quick, clean, and contained flame. Scatter the chopped lemon peel on top of the rosemary.

To use, light the incense with a match. If you are cleansing your house, open all the doors and windows and walk counterclockwise around every room. For personal energy cleansing, stand outside, place the incense dish at your feet, and close your eyes, allowing the smoke to collect and carry away toxic energy.

The greater the clarity and concentration you bring to bear, the more powerful your ritual will be.

SECRET SMOKE SIGNALS: DIVINATION USING INCENSE

Most witches use a pendulum for quick answers to questions that come up in need of a yes or no answer. Burning incense can bring you the same clarity through the ancient divination practice of libanomancy. In libanomancy, we observe and interpret incense smoke.

Begin by setting your intention toward getting an answer to a specific question. Focus on this question and, while standing at your altar, light the incense while holding your query in your mind. Now, pay close attention to the smoke arising from the incense.

- Smoke rising straight up is a yes.
- If the smoke starts to break up and scatter into pieces, this is a no.
- Rings of smoke is also a yes, but with the caution that things will not go as you hope.
- Smoke moving to the right is a sign of great luck.
- Smoke moving to the left signals lack of success and a coming loss.
- Smoke cutting off and dividing at the top is a warning of trouble to come.

Chapter 3

TIME-TESTED TONICS:
A Cup of Contentment

Years ago, I worked with a multinational corporation where I traveled a lot and managed a large department. I guzzled coffee, often two or more triple lattes a day, to keep me going. The more coffee I consumed, the less water and tea I drank. It is amazing that I didn't dry up and blow away. I bought into the corporate "work as many hours as you can" philosophy, and looking back, I can see how unhealthy it was, but at the time I was living in my head and not my body. After a few months, I was waking up every day feeling stressed out and a little unhappier with each passing morning, so I finally stepped off the hamster wheel. One of the first things I did was learn from herbalists and experiment with different teas and healing drinks. I found I was deeply dehydrated and needed to mend my ways. Gone was the daily coffee—down to weekends only—and I excitedly explored the whole realm of natural libations, which is endlessly fascinating and so very nurturing. These are now some of the biggest joys of my life: pots of tea, excursions into the kitchen garden, new combinations of flowers and herbs, and the abundant gifts of Mother Nature's apothecary.

SOUL-SOOTHING TEA SPELL

The pace and pressures of daily life, not to mention the incoming news, can take a toll. We can become ungrounded and lose our center due to the stressors from the outer world, which calls for reconnecting to nature through herbal remedies. This gentlest of teas belies the great strength of this combination to restore both body and soul.

Gather together

Teakettle filled with freshly drawn water

2 tablespoons dried chamomile

1 tablespoon dried catnip

1 tablespoon dried lemon balm

Large tea ball or small muslin bag

Teapot

1 sprig fresh mint

Mug

While the kettle is on the boil, add the herbs to the bag or tea ball and speak this blessing:

Herbs of the goddess, replenish me this day.

Water of the river, restore me this way.

I reclaim my tranquility now, I say.

Blessed be to all. Blessings to me.

Pour the boiled water into the teapot and let steep for 5 minutes to get the full power of these mildest herbs. Take the fresh mint sprig and crush it in the bottom of the mug to release the pure essence of the plant. Pour a cup of the tea and speak the blessing once more. Now sip slowly, making sure to take in the stillness and serenity the brew offers. I have gotten into the habit of drinking more than one mugful in a sitting, and I recommend the same for you. Anytime you need to regain your center and calm, this tea is a sure path to peace of mind.

YIN AND YANG RITE

Did you know that three cups of herbal tea each day not only offers you tranquility but also a marvelous boost to heart and liver health, as well as better sleep and moods? Simply put, drinking a big pot of tea each day is one of the easiest and best things you can do for yourself. Therefore, I suggest dedicating a sacred space to this rite you should observe often. The gift this tea brings us is that of fire and water, combining the energies of yang and yin.

Gather together

3 comfy and colorful pillows

Small low table

Single orchid

Japanese incense, such as plum blossom or jasmine

Fireproof dish or incense burner

Large ceramic teapot and cup

Japanese green tea

Find the most comfortable place in your home and place the pillows on the floor. Set up the low table for taking tea each day and establish a peaceful environment with no clutter. Place the orchid and incense on the table—a light and clean scented Japanese incense is the perfect energetic balancer and cleanser.

Steep some freshly brewed tea in your big pot and set it on the small table beside the flower. Light the incense, place it in the burner, and settle back on the pillows. Sit for three minutes with your eyes closed, breathing in the lightly floral scent of the incense. Clear your mind; think of nothing outside of this moment. Taking tea in this ritualized style helps keep everything in balance for you—it allows you to escape the material world for a time, and then return, refreshed and rebalanced.

FULL MOON TEA

It amuses me to see how trendy cold-brewed tea has become as hedgewitches and wise women have been making this delightful concoction for centuries. It is made in the same way as Sun Tea, which is gently heated by the warmth of the sun, but is brewed at night in the light of the moon.

Gather together

1-quart (1-liter) canning jar with lid

Cold, pure spring water

4 herbal teabags or 3 heaping tablespoons of dried herbs of your choice

Large tea ball or small muslin bag (if using dried herbs)

Fill the jar with the spring water and add the herbal teabags (or the tea ball/muslin bag filled with the dried herbs). Seal the lid on the canning jar and leave it outside or on your windowsill so it can be exposed to the light of the moon. When you awaken in the morning, you will have cold-brewed tea. Do make notes in your Book of Shadows for which brews taste best to you. I can tell you that when the full moon is in the signs of Taurus, Cancer, Virgo, Libra, or Pisces, the tea is most delicious to me, with my current favorites being ginger peach and cinnamon hibiscus.

Herbs for Full Moon Tea

Here are a few suggestions for herbs and plants to use for your Full Moon Tea, as well as Sun Tea and traditional tea.

Beautiful blue borage
This sweetly blue flower has long been used to decorate cakes and other sweets, but also has a light and pleasant flavor that makes for a lovely, fruity tea. You might want to grow borage in your garden because it attracts pollinators such as bees. Borage tea is very calming and is a marvelous anti-inflammatory.

Delicious dandelion
The gardener's bane should actually be greeted gladly, as these humble yellow weeds are superfoods! They make a hearty and healthy tea, and are excellent as salad greens, so you can take advantage of all the nutrients. If that was not enough, dandelions can also be used to make excellent wine!

Helpful hyssop

Both the beautiful purple flowers of hyssop and its leaves have a tangy licorice flavor. This true medicinal can be used from stem to leaf to flower for brewing soothing teas to relieve pain, quiet respiratory complaints, and support your digestion.

Noble nasturtiums

These are one of my favorites, because anyone can grow them anywhere. They reseed themselves, so you only need to plant them once and you will have a salad green, a spicy tea, and gorgeous flowers that cheer you up every time you see them. The leaves of the sun-colored flower can be dried and brewed in a tea that is packed with vitamin C and is capable of both healing and preventing colds and flu.

Loveliest lavender

So versatile, this herb is an absolute necessity in healing magic. While it is nearly universally used as an oil, lotion, and aromatic, it is often forgotten that it makes for a terrific tea. Add bergamot and you will get both an energy boost and a sense of calm. In this case, just breathing in the scent of lavender tea will bring serenity and wellbeing.

Radiant rose

I have an old-fashioned rose with gorgeous orange blossoms that has a tangy scent that is spectacular. Flavors

vary depending on the variety and growing conditions, so petals can be both spicy and sweet, but in general darker petals have more flavor. Brewed into a tea and sweetened with honey, rose will attract love into your life and a sense of self-love as well. The scent and energy of rose is very gentle and will raise your vibration and uplift your personal energy.

Vivid violet

This tea might be the most unusual of all, as it has an enchanted color and can be used to brew a lovely blue-green tea that helps with pain relief, insomnia, and coughs. Johnny jump-ups and their cousin pansy can be used as well. Utterly charming and good for you, too!

HEDGEWITCH HEALING: MAKING HERBAL TINCTURES

Tinctures have been used for millennia and are considered precious because they are so powerful. Tinctures are concentrated liquid extracts of herbs and are taken by the dropperful, most often diluted in warm water or juice. Because they are so potent, they should be administered carefully and sparingly. For chronic problems, add ½ to 1 teaspoon of a tincture to a glass of warm water or juice three times daily. Any of the healing herbs in this book that you feel can help you can be made into tinctures with this easy recipe. The healthful benefits of the herb you select are magnified when adapted into a tincture. There are several methods used to make tinctures, but the simplest method is the one I prefer.

Gather together

6 ounces (170 g) fresh herbs, finely chopped

1-quart (1-liter) sealable jar, such as a Mason jar

26 fluid ounces (750 ml) solvent

Choosing a solvent

Most tinctures are made with alcohol as the primary solvent. Although the amount of alcohol is very small, many people choose not to use alcohol-based tinctures for a variety of sound reasons, and excellent tinctures can be made with apple cider vinegar as the solvent. If you use alcohol, it should be 80- to 100-proof and the best options are vodka, gin, or brandy. Half of the proof number is the percentage of alcohol in the spirits: for example, 80-proof brandy is 40 percent alcohol; 100-proof vodka is 50 percent alcohol.

Herbs to use

Fresh herbs are usually used because they have much more potency, with a ratio of 1 part plant material to 4 parts liquid. If it is winter and only dry herbs are available, use 1 part dried plant material to 1 part liquid, though you may need some extra liquid to cover the herbs. Some marvelously witchy herbs for tinctures are suggested opposite.

Add the herbs to the jar. Pour in the solvent, making sure to cover the herbs with an extra 3 inches (7.5 cm) of liquid above them. Seal the jar tightly. Place the jar in a sunny and warm corner, such as on a windowsill. Keep there for at least a month—up to 6 weeks is ideal. Every day give the mixture a good shake.

Once you're ready, open the jar and strain through a clean, dry muslin or cheesecloth. Once well-strained, pour the remaining liquid into a small bottle or jar and store in a dark cupboard on a high shelf out of the reach of children. The strained herbs will make an excellent compost and this new brew will last nearly indefinitely.

PERFECT PICKS: HERBS FOR TINCTURES

All of us have particular affinities with certain plants, herbs, spices, and flowers. Experiment with each of your astrological tinctures until you find your favorite and the one that offers the most benefits to you.

• Aries herbs are clove, cumin, fennel, juniper, and peppermint.

• Taurus herbs are apple, rose, thyme, tonka bean, vanilla, and violet.

• Gemini herbs are mint, clover, dill, lavender, lemongrass, and parsley.

• Cancer herbs are lemon, lotus, and rose.

• Leo herbs are cinnamon, heliotrope, nutmeg, orange, and rosemary.

• Virgo herbs are almond, mint, and thyme.

• Libra herbs are marjoram, mugwort, spearmint, and sweet pea.

• Scorpio herbs are allspice, basil, cumin, galangal, and ginger.

• Sagittarius herbs are anise, star anise, and honeysuckle.

• Capricorn herbs are lemon thyme, lime, mimosa, and vervain.

• Aquarius herbs are citron, lavender, and spearmint.

• Pisces herbs are clover, blood orange, sarsaparilla, and sweet pea.

ELDERBERRY WISDOM BLEND

One cup of this per day will help you sleep, alleviate anxiety, help aches and pains, and sharpen your mind. Elderberry as a medicinal was especially prized by Druids, who studied flora deeply and regarded elderberry as a holy tree.

Gather together

2 teaspoons dried elderberries

2 teaspoons dried hawthorn berries

1 teaspoon fresh blackberries

1 teaspoon dried raspberry leaf

Small bowl

Large tea ball or muslin bag

Ceramic teapot

Teakettle and water

Honey, to taste

Place all the berries and herbs into the bowl and mix well. Place in a large tea ball or a clean and dry muslin bag in the ceramic teapot. Bring your teakettle to a boil, pour the water over the herbs, and let steep for five minutes. Sweeten to taste with honey—clover honey is especially good. Speak this chant before you drink:

Spirits of nature, bless these herbs,

So we may never be unwell.

Spirits of the Harvest, bless this brew,

So we may leave all worry and woe.

And so it is.

SPICY ROSE HIPS TONIC

We all love rose blossoms but what remains after the petals are long gone is just as good and bursting with vitamin C. Adding other healthful herbs to them makes this drink a delightful energy and wellness boost.

Gather together

4 parts dried rose hips

2 dried rose geranium leaves

2 parts dried dandelion leaves

1 chopped cinnamon stick

Mixing bowl

Sealable jar, such as a Mason jar

Simply mix all the herbs gently in the bowl, then transfer to the jar. This excellent tea can be placed into your tea ball or small muslin cloth for an invigorating brew that will put the bloom of the rose on your cheek!

Enjoy the abundant gifts of Mother Nature's apothecary.

CHICORY ROOT CHEER

I love triple lattes, but they keep me awake into the night and then, in order to function well in the morning, I have to get back on the coffee grind to keep going. Chicory has a similarly wonderful flavor to coffee, but it is caffeine-free and easier on the system. It is a commonly found bright blue wildflower, a member of the daisy family, but it is the parsnip-like roots that are what we use for roasting and grinding. You can find chicory roots at any natural grocery and might become such a fan that you will take a long break from coffee.

Gather together

Bunch of fresh
organic chicory

Sharp knife

Roasting pan

Clean, dry cloth

Coffee grinder

Coffee maker

Mug

Milk and/or sugar, to taste

Preheat the oven to 325°F/170°C/Gas 3. Rinse the chicory roots well in cool water. Cut them into small cubes and let dry on the cloth. Once the roots are dry, place them on the roasting pan and heat for a half hour. Toward the end of the cooking time, you should smell a delightful coffee-like scent. Take out the roasted roots and let them cool. Grind the root pieces like you would coffee beans and brew. I suggest you try your first cup of chicory coffee plain, so you taste the true earthy flavor of the root. In addition to giving your body a break from the stress of caffeine, chicory is very good for detoxing and is less well-known for its magical properties of strength, good luck, frugality, and the removal of obstacles and curses.

BRAIN AND BODY BOOSTER

We all need a pick-me-up once in a while, especially by the end of the week when our physical and emotion tank might be empty. This wild and spicy brew will soon have you moving and grooving again!

Gather together

Teakettle

1 quart (1 liter) freshly drawn water

2 teaspoons fresh nettle

½ teaspoon ginkgo

1 teaspoon fresh or dried licorice

1 teaspoon shopped cinnamon stick

1 teaspoon finely diced ginger root

Mortar and pestle

1-quart (1-liter) sealable jar, such as a Mason jar

While you are boiling the water in the kettle, place the herbs into your mortar and grind them together until well mixed. Transfer the ground herbs to the jar and pour in the boiling water. Steep for a half hour, then strain. The yield should be enough for three big glasses. I suggest you drink one glass while still warm and store and refrigerate the rest in the jar.

The recommended dose per day is three glasses a day in the morning, lunchtime, and after dinner, twice a week. If you are feeling really run down, drink it every other day and you'll pep up quite soon!

THE HOMELY ART OF HERBAL INFUSIONS

I heartily approve of the renewed popularity of these healthful libations. Infusions are derived from the more fragile parts of plants, which include the bud, flower, leaves, and scent-producing parts. These delicate herbs require steeping rather than boiling or simmering. They actually release their flavor more quickly than tougher roots and barks.

Gather together

1 tablespoon herbs of your choice (see list opposite)

Heat-resistant glass bowl

1 cup (240 ml) water

Teakettle

Mug

Add the herbs to the bowl. Boil the water, pour it over the herbs, and let steep for 30 to 60 minutes. Strain into a mug, then enjoy either at room temperature or reheated.

The proportion of water to herb and the required time to infuse varies greatly, depending on the herb. Start out with the above proportions and then experiment. The more herb you use and the longer you let it steep, the stronger the brew. Let your intuition and taste preference be your guide.

HERBS THAT HELP

- Mint sends anxiety and stress away and also calms your stomach.

- Thyme helps with letting go and overcoming grief and clears the lungs.

- Mullein is a wonderful aid for sleep and simple relaxing.

- Sage is renowned for clearing energy, but also tames tension and abets longevity.

- Chamomile makes for sweet sleep and helps you attain a meditative state.

- Nettle settles digestive ills, aches, and pains, while also enhancing psychic powers.

- Oat straw is a brain booster, helps reduce stress, and is a lesser-known love potion!

- Echinacea is known for curing colds, but it can also raise mood, immunity, and prosperity.

- Lavender is a beloved therapeutic, but also brings mental strength and visionary thinking.

- Comfrey is good for bones and skin renewal and will protect both you and your home.

Witchy curative concoctions

Wellness can and should be easy. It shouldn't stress us out to manage our stress, right? Try making a simple tea using one of the herbs listed below. Keep it simple by using one tablespoon of your chosen herb for every quart (liter) of hot water. Steep for at least 30 minutes, or 45 minutes if you like stronger brews. Strain, then serve or store. Keep notes in your Book of Shadows or self-care journal regarding what works best for you. I am often surprised and still find it thrilling that chicory is a real energy herb for me. When you've found what works, stick with it!

For purifying: Dandelion greens, lemon balm, or nettle leaves

For less stress: Astragalus, dandelion root, or ginseng

For calm breath: Ginger root, licorice root, or marshmallow root

For improved mood: Ginger root, lemon balm, or rose hips

For women's wellness: Ginger root, peppermint, or red raspberry leaf

For good sleep: Chamomile, lavender, or thyme

MEDICINAL MAGIC

Herbal tea is truly a mainstay for wellbeing and has been for millennia. Brewing every morning can even be a deeply pleasant way to begin each day, as it is for me. I mix it up a few times each week in accordance with what I sense I will need for the day. Keep notes about what works for you and, after a while, you should have a good supply of different herbal teas you know bring you health and happiness. I usually brew a large pot of tea and it can last through the day, going from hot in the morning to iced in the afternoon. Don't let your tea sit out at room temperature for too long, as it will go "flat," get tiny bubbles in it, and begin to sour. When stored in the refrigerator, an herbal tea will be good for three to four days.

POWERFUL HEALING HERBS

• **Cold calmers:** Echinacea, elderberry, hibiscus, or nettle

• **Headache healers:** Chamomile, clove, peppermint, or willow bark

• **Fever fighters:** Bergamot, catnip, white willow bark, or yarrow

• **Stomach soothers:** Chamomile, fennel, ginger, holy basil, licorice (this is very strong so use only 1 teaspoon per cup of water), or mint

• **Sleep and serenity:** Lavender, lemon balm, lemongrass, passionflower, or valerian

A simple rule of thumb is to use 1–2 tablespoons of herb for each cup (240 ml) of water, or 4–6 tablespoons of herb per quart (liter) of water, unless it is a very strong herb as indicated in the box, left.

For a medicinal tea to be effective, it must be administered in small amounts several times daily. For chronic problems, serve the tea three or four times daily. For acute ailments, such as colds, fevers, and headaches, take several small sips every 30 minutes until the symptoms subside.

GINGER LEMON WINE

For most of us, ginger is our go-to for stomach-settling tea, but wine made from this wholesome root offers the very same benefit. It will also warm you at night and abet easy and peaceful sleep.

Bruise the ginger by mashing it with the wooden spoon in the pan. Add half the water and bring to a slow boil. Stir well and place the lid on the pan. Turn the heat down to simmer for 30 minutes, then remove from the heat and let it cool for ten minutes.

Pour the sugar, lemon juice, and honey into a bowl and stir well with the wooden spoon. Now pour the ginger mixture into the bowl. Boil the remaining water, add to the bowl, and stir until the sugar is completely dissolved and all is thoroughly mixed. Now strain the liquid back into the pan and then again back into the bowl.

Pour the strained ginger lemon liquid into the bottle and label it. For example, if the moon is new and in the sign of Gemini, add that to your label so it reads: Gemini New Moon Ginger Lemon Wine. Let it set for 24 hours and, after that, it is good to go. Drink it chilled or warm for an inner glow.

Gather together

½ cup (50 g) fresh ginger, chopped

Large lidded pan

Wooden spoon

2 gallons (7.5 liters) fresh water

5 cups (1 kg) granulated sugar

Juice of 3 lemons

½ cup (125 ml) honey

Large bowl

Strainer

Large corked bottle

Label and pen

HOME-BREWED APPLE CIDER VINEGAR

Sometimes I think that I didn't so much choose my home but that the tree in the backyard chose me. We are true companions and I have learned much from my beloved tree, which is one of the few remaining of an apple orchard from the 1800s. It is truly goddess-blessed land, watched over by Pomona, the apple goddess. Every autumn is a bountiful harvest, letting nothing go to waste. After the best apples are used to make pies, anything left over is perfect for making apple cider and the accompanying vinegar. There are many devotees to apple cider vinegar as it is one of nature's most effective remedies; it is antioxidant and excellent as an immune booster, for weight loss, and for abetting digestive issues, for starters.

Gather together

1 pound (500 g) apples, rinsed, chopped, organic, and pesticide-free

1-quart (1-liter) canning jar with sealable lid and ring, such as a Mason jar, clean and sterilized

¼ cup (50 g) sugar

½ quart (500 ml) freshly boiled water

2 coffee filters

2 clean rubber bands

Bowl

Fill the jar with the chopped apples, then add the sugar. Pour in the hot water to the very top of the canning jar. Cover the lid with the jar ring and a coffee filter secured by a rubber band. Store the jar out of direct sunlight but on a warm shelf—beside a refrigerator is a perfect spot and the slight warmth will speed up the fermentation process.

After just a few days, the apple mixture will begin to bubble and foam. After two weeks, strain the liquid into a bowl, clean the jar, then refill the jar with the strained liquid. Cover exactly as before using a coffee filter, canning jar ring, and rubber band. Store on the same warm shelf.

After another two weeks, the liquid will appear cloudy and a film will form on the surface which you should skim off. This is referred to as the "mother" and can be used as a starter for future cider vinegars. Just refrigerate and add a tablespoon of mother into a clean canning jar that has a cup of water in it.

Six weeks from the start, your fermentation process will be complete and the apple cider vinegar is ready to use. Apple cider vinegar can keep for two years and it is not necessary to store it in the refrigerator unless you prefer it chilled. Keep records in your Book of Shadows so you learn which moon signs and phases work best for you when making it. You should be brewing up a batch of apple cider vinegar at least once a year and, over time, you will perfect yours.

Herbal healing vinegars

In addition to apple cider vinegar, I recommend building a pantry shelf of different herbal vinegars—they are a constant delight and do not taste medicinal. Nevertheless, they contain the healing properties and magical energies of the plants they are made from. Imbibing a little each day is wonderful for women in particular, as a mere tablespoon has the same amount of calcium as a glass of milk. You can also add herbal vinegars to salad dressings, soups, stews, and other savory dishes for a dash of bright flavor.

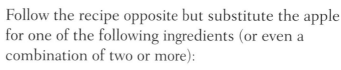

Follow the recipe opposite but substitute the apple for one of the following ingredients (or even a combination of two or more):

Use the leaves and stalks: Apple mint, catnip, garlic, mustard, orange mint, peppermint, rosemary, and thyme

Use the roots: Burdock, chicory, dandelion, ginger, and mugwort

Use the flowers: Chives, dandelion, goldenrod, lavender, and yarrow

Use the seeds: Dill and fennel

POMONA'S MULLING MAGIC: HOT CIDER

For any high holiday or sabbat festival, this is a blessed brew that will not only create conviviality but also imbue your home with a heaven-sent fragrance.

Gather together

1 gallon (4.5 liters) apple cider

Large stockpot

Peel of half an orange, cut into pieces

1 heaping teaspoon ginger root, diced

2 star anise pods

3 cinnamon sticks, cut in half

1 tablespoon whole cloves

Muslin bag and string to tie

Pour the cider into the pot and place on a low heat. Put the orange peel and the spices into the muslin bag and tie with a string. Now add the spice bundle into the pot and let simmer to a slow boil. Once the brew has reached a rolling boil, turn off the heat and serve delightful and delicious mugs full of magic.

Prayer to Pomona

We should always express gratitude to the deities who come to our aid. My guardian goddess, Pomona, is the goddess of orchards and apples and a protector of women. She can be your protector, too.

Speak the following words after your daily dose of apple cider vinegar or after sipping a cup of hot cider:

She of sylvan hills who watches over,

Keep us safe, keep us whole.

Accept this prayer of thanks

For your abundant wisdom

And generosity in gratitude eternal.

She of sylvan hills who watches over,
keep us safe, keep us whole.

Chapter 4

KITCHEN ALCHEMY:
Nourishing Body and Soul

A good friend of mine swears by a spa she visited years ago high in the mountains of Germany. At first it sounded glamorous, but as I heard more, I realized it was also very practical and old-fashioned with practices from centuries ago, including salt scrubs, floral waters, herbal baths, tea and elixirs, therapeutic oil rubs, and other restorative rites. These traditions had been handed down from Bavarian hedgewitches and village elders. Why do people fly to Europe for healing retreats and spa treatments? Because they work! Yet many of these tried and tested recipes and rituals can be whipped up right in your own kitchen using botanicals from your kitchen garden, herb pots on your deck or windowsill, and local greengrocer and apothecary. Once you have dabbled in your own inspired alchemy, I know this will become one of your chief pleasures in life. By concocting your self-care solutions, you will have a sense of groundedness in the sanctity of your life and your connection to nature and the world.

VANILLA BEAN VITALITY BATH

Vanilla has the power to comfort and cheer, but it also has the spirit of love and raises energy and liveliness. This excellent combination can create an amorous and uplifting feeling.

Gather together

Whole vanilla bean

Glass jar with lid or cork closure

1 cup (240 g) Epsom salts

4 drops of vanilla extract

Mixing bowl and wooden spoon

Put the vanilla bean into the glass jar. Put the salts in the bowl, add the drops of vanilla extract, and fold in thoroughly. Transfer the salt mixture into the jar and let sit overnight until the morning while the vanilla bean infuses into the salts.

To use, add the entire contents of the jar as you run a hot bath. Make sure to add the bean pod to the bath, too, for the full dose of high heart energy. Save this bath for a very special occasion, such as before a big date.

DEEP SLEEP HERBAL IMMERSION

If you have been restive, this aromatic, therapeutic immersion will have you in a deep slumber. The combination of herbs provides real calm.

Combine the Epsom salts and baking soda in the bowl with the wooden spoon and then add the essential oils and blend well. This makes enough for 4 baths. Store in the sealable jar for whenever you need a respite from the worries of the world.

Gather together

1 cup (240 g) Epsom salts

1 cup (240 g) baking soda (bicarbonate of soda)

Mixing bowl and wooden spoon

12 drops clary sage essential oil

12 drops lavender essential oil

8 drops jasmine essential oil

Sealable jar or canister

ROSE RITUAL MILK BATH

Rose petals and essential oil are both abundant in practices of self-love and self-care. Making potions at home for yourself will also raise your vibration to a higher level, which is healthy in every way. Soaking in this rose petal milk bath is as soul-soothing as it is skin-soothing.

Put the salts in the bowl and stir in the powdered milk. Add the essential oils and stir in the rose petals. Start running the bath and spoon the bath mixture under the faucet. Both the flowers and the milk powder will rehydrate you in a flower-filled steam and create a heavenly perfumed vibration for this ritual. Speak aloud:

From paradise garden eternal

Comes the sweetness of rose.

From the water of heaven eternal

The source of all love flows.

Blessed be me; and so it is.

Gather together

1 cup (240 g) Epsom salts

Bowl and wooden spoon

2 cups (150 g) powdered milk

6 drops rose essential oil

½ cup (10 g) dried rose petals

½ cup (120 ml) almond carrier oil

HERBAL SPA STEAM

Several healing traditions, including European and Native American, consider steams and saunas to be a vital part of life-long wellness for "sweating out" toxins from your body through your skin. There is no need to start building a sauna in your house—there is an easier way that costs little and is invaluable as a method of cleansing toxins.

Gather together

2 cups fresh herbs
(see suggestions below)

5-gallon (19-liter) stockpot
(optional)

In your bathroom, add the fresh herbs to the stockpot and carefully fill it with boiling hot water. (If you do not have a stockpot, you could put the herbs in your bathtub and fill that with hot water instead.) Sit on a stool or bench beside it, sans any clothes, breathe in the steam, and enjoy the warm air and nurturing aromas of the botanicals. This home steam can be performed once a month.

Herbs for your home spa

Choose from the list below for your perfect home steam. You can also mix the herbs, and I recommend lemon peel and chamomile for a soothing team.

- Comfrey is an astringent and boosts skin refreshing.
- Lemon peel is excellent for the respiratory system and uplifts your mood.
- Calendula is an anti-inflammatory and skin soother.
- Chamomile helps with dry skin and is calming.
- Peppermint is wonderful for the lungs and improving your mood.
- Eucalyptus leaf vapor is mightily restorative and helps ease headaches.

HEALTHY IS BEAUTIFUL: EASY DIY SALT RUB

Healthy skin glows, but it doesn't happen all by itself. Drinking lots of water and herbal tea helps, as does a good salt rub. Many of us practical witches prefer concocting our own healing beauty magic. Here's a simple recipe for a homemade salt rub. The beauty of this recipe is that you can change the essential oils to suit your mood. Cinnamon oil adds a pleasing tingle to this treatment and is a lesser-known healthy skin essential oil.

Add all the ingredients to the bowl and mix well. Transfer to the glass jar for storage—this makes enough for three baths. It also makes a thoughtful gift for friends and fellow pagans.

To use, measure out 1 cup (240 g) of the salt mixture, then set aside 1 tablespoon of this cup onto the loofah or washcloth. When the tub is one-quarter full, add the rest of the cup under the faucet as the hot water flows out. When the tub is full, step in and breathe in deeply ten times, inhaling and exhaling fully before you recite these words:

Healing waters and salt of this earth

Remove from me any impurities

Of the body, spirit, and mind.

As you cleanse my body,

I ask for renewal

Of body, soul, and mind.

So mote it be.

Gently exfoliate your skin with the loofah or washcloth while in the bath.

Gather together

3 cups (720 g) Epsom salts

1 tablespoon carrot seed essential oil

6 drops clary sage essential oil

2 drops jasmine essential oil

2 drops cinnamon essential oil

Large mixing bowl and wooden spoon

Large dark glass jar with lid

Loofah or clean, dry washcloth

MANGO GROVE MASSAGE BUTTER BARS

As we all know, our skin is our single largest organ. Therefore, taking good care of your skin is important by drinking enough water, ideally at least 8 cups (2 liters) of water a day, as well as hydrating your skin with the right kind of lotions and moisturizer. It should not clog your skin or pores and chemical-laden products can do that. Keep it natural. Mango butter is made from the fruit kernels of the mango tree and is sumptuous. This recipe was created to remind us of the divine fragrance of a fruit grove, and will elevate your spirit as well.

Gather together

3 ounces (85 g) beeswax

3 fluid ounces (90 ml) apricot oil

3 ounces (85 g) mango butter

Double-boiler pan and wooden spoon

1 teaspoon neroli essential oil

4 soap bar molds or a muffin tin

Begin by slowly heating the beeswax, apricot oil, and mango butter in your double-boiler pan over low heat until it has just melted and then take off the heat. After letting cool for a few minutes, add the neroli essential oil into the mixture and stir with the wooden spoon. Carefully pour into the soap molds or four of the holes in the muffin tin and cool in the refrigerator for an hour or until hardened. I keep one of my refrigerator drawers filled with homemade massage bars like these, as well as soaps and lotions, so I always have enough to share with friends.

These bars feel luxurious to the skin and are excellent for relaxing and applying to aching shoulders, sore knees, and anywhere that needs a healing touch. They are wonderfully therapeutic for massaging friends and loved ones, but you can also use them on yourself. A friend of mine uses the ones I gave to her as a moisturizer and loves the smell and silky-smooth results.

FARMER'S MARKET FACIAL MASKS

Many of the fruits and veggies we love cooking and eating also make for splendid home-spa treatments, as they contain acids that gently exfoliate your skin and imbue your life with magic. Ten minutes is the ideal time to leave the mask on to avoid any dryness and fully refresh.

Avocado smooth

This luxurious fruit is packed with vitamins A, B, D, and E and potassium, along with smoothing oils, and is truly wonderful for the skin, adding much moisture. Half an avocado mashed all by itself and allowed to dry as a mask is good enough, but if you blend in some honey, it exfoliates as it nurtures. In witchcraft, this fruit is regarded as an aphrodisiac and also as good for making peace.

Strawberry fields

Strawberries contain natural salicylic acid, which can gently remove impurities. ½ cup (50 g) mashed strawberries and ½ cup (50 g) cornstarch (cornflour) mixed together is also filled with antioxidants—simply apply to your face and neck to get the benefits. These berries are imbued with love and luck magic and are especially linked to women's wellness.

Peach perfect protection

Simply bursting with vitamins A and C, peaches nourish and brighten the skin, and the naturally-found alpha-hydroxyl acid in the fruit hydrates. One mashed peach blended with 1 tablespoon each of oatmeal and honey is a simple mask that will refresh your skin and also add the energy of protection provided by peaches. This stone fruit contains longevity magic along with romance.

Blackberry cream

These beauties brighten your skin thanks to the combination of certain enzymes and vitamin C. They are renowned antioxidants and can be made into a pomade when mashed and mixed with plain yogurt, using ¼ cup of each (130 g blackberries and 215 g yogurt). Smooth it onto your face, neck, and décolletage and let sit. Shower it off (you may need to wipe with a washcloth, too, to remove all residue) and you'll look and feel much fresher. Fairies love blackberries and they also bring the magic of grounding and make connections closer.

TEA LEAF TONER MIST

Having this bracingly minty toner on hand will be an enchanting refresher whenever you need it.

Gather together

2 teaspoons peppermint leaves

2 teaspoons white sage tea

French press (cafétière)

½ cup (120 ml) boiled distilled water

3 drops lavender essential oil

4 fluid ounces (110 ml) aloe vera gel

6-fluid ounce (170-ml) spray bottle

Place the peppermint and tea leaves into the French press and then pour the freshly boiled water over the herbs. Let steep for 10 minutes, then add the lavender essential oil drops. Pour the aloe vera gel into the spray bottle, followed by the warm herbal tea, and seal the bottle. Shake well and refrigerate.

Anytime you need a mood shift or to feel restored, spritz the mist on your face, and even your arms and legs. You will feel refreshed instantly.

APPLE CIDER VINEGAR ABLUTIONS

Did you know your home-brewed apple cider vinegar (see page 56) could be a beauty aid, too?

• Tonic toner: Apple cider vinegar is naturally antiseptic and is marvelous at regulating your skin's pH levels and calming inflammation. Pour a little into your palms and splash all over your face and neck. It is very soothing and tones your skin, leaving it smooth and soft.

• Tangle tamer: Everything apple cider vinegar does for your skin, it does for your hair, as well as helping to detangle it. A friend of mine has given up all store-bought shampoos and conditioners and uses only apple cider vinegar variations. She points out that the chemical residue from store-bought shampoo and over-conditioning weigh down hair and make it dull. She's right! For healthy and very shiny hair, use 1 cup (240 ml) apple cider vinegar diluted with an equal part of distilled water and pour it directly onto the top of your head before rinsing out in the shower.

HEALING DOSES OF COLOR

Color has a profound effect on our psychological and physical health. Consider carefully the colors that surround you, because each of us has special colors that encourage a sound body and mind. For example, if you have a weight issue and lack ambition or energy, you may need more orange in your life. Wear orange clothes and eat foods associated with orange, such as red plums and wax beans.

Color connections

- Red, associated with aggression, success, and control, is best absorbed through cabbage, bacon, cherries, lemons, tomatoes, and paprika.
- Orange, associated with abundance and ebullience, can be absorbed through oranges, squash, red plums, yeast, and wax beans.
- Yellow is connected to renown, wealth, power, and excellence, and is best ingested through pumpkin, cheese, rye, oats, lettuce, and beer.

- Green, the color of everlasting life, friendship, and optimism, is concentrated in beef, alfalfa, endive, and grapes.
- Blue relates to humility, faith, and innocence, and is the mainstay of mint, garlic, radishes, sage, turnips, and peppers.
- Violet is associated with sentiment, melancholy, and religious devotion, and can be enhanced by eating chocolate, thyme, and scallops.

ANCIENT SECRETS TO RADIANCE

To strengthen your vivacity and vitality and prompt the highest of spirits, this incense enhanced with essential oils will do it. It brings forth the greatest result if burned during the full moon phase.

Gather together

1 teaspoon myrrh incense

1 teaspoon sandalwood incense

1 teaspoon frankincense incense

Mortar and pestle

3 drops sandalwood essential oil

3 drops frankincense essential oil

3 drops amber essential oil

Fireproof dish and charcoal wafer

Start by grinding all the incense in your mortar and pestle until they are mixed together. Add the essential oils and grind again lightly. Cover the charcoal wafer in your fireproof dish with the mixture and light the incense. Silently speak the following spell:

Under this moon in this night,

With every word, I draw down delight.

With every breath, I feel the light.

Tonight, this moon grows more bright.

Tonight, I embrace life with all my might,

So mote it be.

Let the incense burn for as long as you wish.

ESSENCE OF WELLNESS

This homemade healing oil brings an instant immune system boost. As soon as you feel slightly rundown, one application should make a difference.

Gather together

¼ cup (10 g) dried rosemary

¼ cup (10 g) crushed sandalwood chips

¼ cup (10 g) fresh carnation petals

Mortar and pestle

Sealable colored glass jar

Extra-virgin olive oil

Crush the rosemary, sandalwood, and carnation petals in the mortar. Transfer the crushed herbs to the jar and fill it with olive oil, making sure to cover the herbs. Store for seven days on a windowsill where the jar will be exposed to both the sun and moon. Strain the oil, then return the infused oil to the jar.

You now have a hearty supply of oil to use in the bath, or to rub on your pulse points: on your temples, wrists, and neck and behind the ears.

Chapter 5

GROWING BLESSINGS:
Herbs, Flowers, and Trees

One of the greatest pleasures in my life is my garden, and it is a place where I gain peace of mind, great solace, and simple happiness. I work from home part of the time and in between video meetings and calls, I run out to do some weeding and check on seedlings, budding lemons, and how new plantings are doing. Even if I have just been somewhat stressed by a tight deadline, the minute I step into sweet and verdant space, I immediately feel at ease and literally start breathing more easily. I joke to people that weeding is my therapy, but it is pretty accurate. Over and above the daily delights of nurturing plants both inside and outside your home, you can be intentional about how your garden grows and bring magic, healing, and protection to you and your loved ones by growing plants that contain those inherent powers. This chapter reveals some of the secrets I learned from my Aunt Edith, who had the greenest of thumbs, and from other wise women who generously shared their sacred wisdom.

CLEANSING CONJURATION

Before you begin cultivating your magic garden, you should remove any negative energy from the soil. We never know what has happened in the previous decades and it is essential to cleanse the land in which you plan to grow herbs, flowers, and veggies; the very ground needs to be purified and blessed with a prayer of health for your plants, yourself, and your home.

Gather together

Large black pillar candle

Large flat rock or tray

Obsidian crystal

Fireproof dish or incense burner

Palo Santo incense

Green bowl filled with water

1 sprig rosemary

Go outside to the area where you are planning to garden and place the pillar candle on the flat rock or tray, then place the black crystal and incense dish alongside it. Light the candle and use the candle flame to light the Palo Santo incense. The candle dispels past negative energies and the obsidian absorbs these vibrations from past unhappy events.

Dip your fingers into the bowl of water and sprinkle drops behind you and in front of you. Then pray aloud:

Gods and goddesses, guardian spirits,

Please cleanse this land and remove what no longer serves.

By my heart and by my hands, I will plant and sow.

Heal this earth and a garden will bloom in joy.

Here will grow happiness; here will grow healing.

Great gratitude to you, the Guardians of the Earth.

So mote it be.

Now take the sprig of rosemary and place a few of the spikey leaves in the incense dish. Rosemary creates one of the most powerful cleansing and purifying smokes. Repeat the prayer and then use the water to put out the incense. Remove all the ritual elements so the earth is as it should be—clean and clear.

MENDING MEDLEY

I prefer herbal and floral potpourri brews to the dried Victorian approach. The bouquet of scents has a quicker and more effective aromatherapeutic impact in my experience. Here's a quick recipe for a blissful brew.

Gather together

½ cup (20 g) dried peppermint

½ cup (20 g) dried orange peel

½ cup (50 g) dried bayberry or dried rose hips

½ cup (10 g) rose petals

6 broken cinnamon sticks

Saucepan and wooden spoon

2 cups (500 ml) distilled water

Place the herbs and spices into the saucepan and pour in the distilled water. Heat slowly and stir gently. While stirring, pray aloud:

Sacred brew of leaf and tree

Fill this home with peace from thee.

As strong as the rooted tree

May all who reside here be.

And so it is.

This brew can be used a few times. When you have finished using it as a potpourri, you can dry it and use it in a ritual fire, where it will waft a healing smoke.

ENCHANTED PLANTINGS

I have mostly lived in small spaces with no outside to speak of bar a deck or fire escape, but tending potted herbs on a windowsill, containers filled with fruit trees, flowering plants, and vines hanging off the balcony brought me deep joy and a sense of connection to nature. I also felt I was serving and helping care for Mother Earth. Nothing is more grounding. You really can garden your way to gladness. So, no matter the space you have available, consider growing some of the following herbs and flowers which are ideal for a witch's garden.

Angelica, guardian angel herb

Hedgewitches have brewed dried angelica as tea since the earliest medieval ages and prized it for healing the stomach and also for stimulating a flagging appetite. It was even said to aid those who were sick during the plague times. Dried angelica root is a protector plant and can be worn for this purpose as well or tucked into your wallet. Grow angelica in your garden to protect your home and to keep away ill spirits looking to create mischief.

Aromatic anise

Anise is another bright-flavored herb of protection and wellness. It offers many culinary options, including simply adding some to spiced cider or wine you are mulling for a digestive hot toddy. If you are experiencing sleep disruptions, place a small pouch of dried

anise seeds under your pillow at night and you will sleep and dream deeply. Anise stands guard and keeps adverse spirits away, and if you are trying to communicate with unseen ancestors, deities, or those who have ascended, anise can enhance seership. Anise is not unlike fennel or licorice when brewed as a tea, in that it brings great calm to digestion, breathing, and any lung issues. It is also very good for women's health and can aid mothers in milk production for nursing. Added to a bath, anise purifies and protects. If you are feeling dull and flat, and lacking joy in your life, anise will brighten moods and raise your vibration and energy level. It also can open your third eye and enhance your intuition.

Fortunate fennel

A delightfully tasty veggie herb, every part of fennel is at your service: seeds, fronds, flowers, and bulbs. Whether included in salad or simply roasted, fennel is an all-purpose herb you'll come to love. It is delicious with a bright and fresh flavor. It is also a sentinel plant that offers security from ill spirits and any bad thoughts aimed your way. It is wonderfully effortless to grow, and once you have it started in your kitchen garden, it will continue to prosper and spread while it stands guard. You can hang fronds in the window to dry or bag seeds as amulets. Growing fennel will bring good fortune to your home. Fennel is a great healer and can be used in tea to soothe your stomach, colds, and flus, and even promote bone strength and boost immunity. Fennel brings you money, luck, protection, health, and good food and drink. Plant some seeds soon!

Ferns are favored by fairies

When you take a walk in a park, forest, or field, you will see myriad kinds of ferns as there are so many and they vary so widely. It is very likely that you will feel drawn to a certain type of fern, so take your time and let it speak to you. You can also browse for them at nurseries and arboretums, as I did. They all provide excellent protection and love to grow nestled up against your home where they can keep negative energy and bad spirits at bay. One witchy tip to try is to fend off thieves or ill-intentioned people from your home by sprinkling fern leaves on the windowsills, or keeping a vase with a single fern leaf on the sill or a fern-filled terrarium on a nearby shelf. Tuck fern leaves into a small bag and wear it as personal protection and, as a double blessing, ferns will protect you from both illness and hexes. As if ferns are not helpful enough, you can add fern leaves to the water before you clean your floors and they will remove any bad energy. No wonder fairies love ferns and seek their shelter and comfort!

Juniper berries bring buoyancy

Juniper berries are not only useful in gin but on their own are also one of the most positive herbs you can keep around you as they ward off unkind thoughts and adverse energies. Whereas mugwort is very intense, juniper berries are gentle in the way they work to negate bad intentions; they simply steer them away. Wise women and witches of yore would string necklaces and bracelets made of juniper berries as protective jewelry.

These berries are good for manifesting what you want in life, including love. Dried berries in a small pouch will attract a new lover to you. They are excellent for deep meditation that engenders calm with a sense of being unburdened, lighter, and refreshed. You could string together a pagan rosary with the berries for times of prayer and contemplation.

Mugwort for mystical visions

Mugwort has long been regarded as an herb sacred to the Triple Goddess, cronehood, and the moon because it is so powerful. It is a divinatory herb and can be used to bring out psychism and invoke visionary states inducing astral travel. Mugwort beer was a favorite in medieval times. It is also a protector herb and, unsurprisingly, can be used to ward off psychic attacks and curses. Many witches sleep with mugwort under their pillow for the protection it provides. Mugwort plants can be bundles, dried and bound together for a broom specially used to sweep any bad energy from your home. Leaves can also be dried and used like sage for smudging. Mugwort wreaths hung on the front door will prevent negative energy from entering your home. By steeping mugwort in hot water, you can make a tonic that offers great calm and is also soothing to the stomach. As an essential oil, it can be rubbed on front doors, windows, your altar, and anywhere you feel the need to be safer and secure. It can also safeguard against injury and preserve your personal strength and vitality.

Rosemary, guardian of the garden

Rosemary was used for smudging long before sage, starting in Mesopotamia where priests and holy women would burn branches of this herb—just as I do when an extra boost is needed for energetic cleaning, in an abalone shell I keep as an incense burner. The smell of burning rosemary is very sharp, exemplifying its power to purge the negative. Rosemary can also be placed in a cloth amulet or in your wallet for personal protection, but it is truly a guardian of the ground and should ideally be planted by the front door to safeguard your home.

With multitudinous magical uses, rosemary brings good luck, love, and peacefulness, and can also be added to salt for cleansing your magical tools. It is a sheer delight in cooking and is an aphrodisiac—perfect for romantic dinners at home. This woody herb was prized by the ancients for its power to bring forth your memories and hone the mind. This plant is a mood booster, too, and the essential oil added to lotions and baths is marvelous for circulation and youthful, glowing skin.

Sage makes the wearer wiser

Sage is a healing herb and as such is renowned for both longevity and fertility and for sharpening the memory and mind. It is one of the very best herbs for protecting and purifying. It is often used in smudging for cleansing smoke and helps rid your home of negative energies, but it is less well known that wearing sage offers personal protection. An easy way is to put some in a little muslin bag to wear as an amulet or to keep some in your wallet or bag. A saying from the days of old is that "sage makes the wearer wiser" and abets meditation greatly.

HEALING TREES TO PLANT NEAR YOUR HOME

• Dogwood offers protection and sitting near a dogwood tree helps deal with grief and loss.

• Sassafras is actually a curative: brewing the bark in tea fends off cold and headaches. It also wards away negative spirits and can increase your prosperity.

• Osage orange wood uplifts and inspires. A fallen branch can be a healing wand that can also be used to call forth spirit guides and animal guardians.

• Pine trees are very healing when used as essential oils and also attract money, will boost your moods, and purify thoughts. Burning the seeds in incense can reverse spells and hexes. Hanging branches increase both magical and curative energies. If you feel bad vibes, you can scatter pine needles around your yard or garden to reject evil.

• Magnolia trees enhance your immune system, lift self-confidence, and remove sorrow. This goddess tree is good for women to have nearby as it makes you stronger of body and mind.

• Palo Santo is a holy wood and one of the finest of clearing incenses. It reduces stress, calms headaches, and alleviates anxiety. Palo Santo removes negative energy and replaces it with positive. It will also inspire and heighten creativity.

• Sandalwood is a wonderfully grounding tree that increases spiritual connection while centering you. It is also a protector and healer. The scent activates something in the mind that should help put you on the path to enlightenment—the vibration is healing and calming.

• Linden tree wands have powerful healing properties and the trees are connected to positivity and light, bright energy. Hedgewitches of old used linden for healing magic with essential oils, wreaths, and branches. It is considered a very magical and medicinal tree.

SYLVAN SPELL: CHOOSING YOUR TREE FAMILIAR

As Druids, Celts, hedgewitches, and J.R. R. Tolkien knew and passed down in lore to us, trees contain powerful magic. Each tree is a being with its own distinct energy. Perhaps you have a grove in your patch when you take a walk and feel drawn to a certain area. Follow that sense and see if it takes you to a certain tree. If so, this tree has chosen you. You can also select a tree that looks special to you in some way, perhaps the trunk has an appealing pattern, or the leaves strike you as particularly fine-looking.

Befriend this tree and it can be your forest familiar. Name your tree and bind it to you with a naming ritual. Try to let the name come to you in a dream, but you can also pick the name, as I did with my first forest familiar from the family farm. I was a Tolkien-loving teen and dubbed an ancient willow Treebeard. Once you have identified your tree, take a small sheaf of paper and write down the name of your newfound familiar. Place this on your altar overnight and visit your tree at first light of dawn. Speak the following spell aloud:

In this dew of morning,

I honor my connection to you,
_____ [say the tree's name]

In this mist of dawn,

I seal my oath to you, _____
[say the tree's name]

This magical bond will serve us both

For the good of all. So mote it be.

Now take the paper with the tree's name and roll it into a scroll. Bury it under one of the tree's shallow roots so it will stay hidden and bond with the soil.

MAGICAL TREES

Here are common trees and their magical associations:

- Apple: healing, Goddess energy, and farming

- Aspen: endurance, good health, and prosperity

- Beech: intuition, creativity, friendship, and security

- Birch: birth, blessings, creativity, crafting, fertility, Goddess energy, healing, inspiration, love, protection, and renewal

- Bottlebrush: abundance, banishing, energy, and love

- Cypress: grieving, healing, longevity, protection, and solace

- Elder: fairies, good fortune, enchantment, and protection

- Elm: compassion, understanding, rest, and wisdom

- Fig: divination, enlightenment, fertility, good luck, and romance

- Hazel: artistry, seership, new knowledge, and protection

- Heather: changes, healing, luck, passion, and spirituality

- Hickory: money, kindness, strength, and transformation

- Holly: courage, protection, rebirth, and unity

- Maple: communication, grounding, and luck in love

- Oak: protection, robustness, strength, success, and intelligence

- Pine: emotions, good luck, protection, purification, and renewal

- Sequoia: enlightenment, eternity, growth, valor, and wisdom

- Spruce: enlightenment, grounding, intuition, and versatility

- Willow: grieving, psychism, relationships, and wishes

WELLNESS WEEDS

Make the most of Mother Nature's medicine cabinet! These classic healing herbs can all be found in your local health store or online.

Ashwagandha (*Withania somnifera*)

Gently simmer 1 tablespoon of dried and minced ashwagandha root in 1 cup (240 ml) water for 8–10 minutes. Strain and sip once or twice a day as a rejuvenating tonic, anti-inflammatory, anxiety reducer, and immunity reducer.

Black cohosh (*Actaea racemosa*)

Make a tincture (see page 46) and take 1–2 milliliters three times a day to relieve menstrual cramps and arthritic pain. Black cohosh can also help peri- and menopausal symptoms.

Calendula (*Calendula officinalis*)

Boil 1 cup (240 ml) water and pour over two teaspoons of calendula petals. Steep this for 8–10 minutes and strain. Once it has cooled enough, you can drink it as tea, or use it as a mouthwash or gargle with it to reduce any swelling of the mouth or throat.

Calendula can also be made into a salve (see page 104) to heal the skin and soothe rashes, itching, irritation, and wounds. Apply to your skin three times a day to calm any irritation. Your family will probably request the comfort of the calendula salve often, so keep it handy.

Elderberry (*Sambucus nigra ssp. canadensis*)

This time-tested medicinal has long been used for guarding against colds and flu. Elderberry flowers have been valued as a tonic for fever for centuries; such fruit extracts have been proven to be noteworthy antivirals, especially against immunity issues. Two teaspoons of dried flowers in 1 cup (240 ml) boiling water three times a day does the trick—sweeten with local honey (see page 84) to taste.

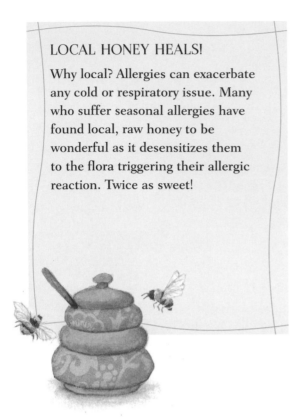

LOCAL HONEY HEALS!

Why local? Allergies can exacerbate any cold or respiratory issue. Many who suffer seasonal allergies have found local, raw honey to be wonderful as it desensitizes them to the flora triggering their allergic reaction. Twice as sweet!

Garlic (*Allium sativum*)

We have all heard that the Chinese praise garlic for the health benefits. It is a powerful antimicrobial, often employed to combat colds, ease sinus congestion, and stave off digestion problems that accompany traveling. It has even been shown that regular use can help gently lower blood pressure. 1–2 fresh cloves are the dose.

Ginger root (*Zingiber officinale*)

From tummy troubles to colds and flus, ginger is beloved for its curative powers. Any greengrocer or herbal apothecary will have plenty of ginger root in stock, which you should always have around. When anyone in your family feels nauseous or a cold or fever coming, slice and mince a tablespoon of the root in 1 cup (240 ml) hot water for tea. Steep to taste and drink twice a day for a surprisingly swift end to your suffering.

Ginseng (*Panax quinquefolius*; *Panax ginseng*)

Many people rely upon ginseng to relieve and avert mental and physical fatigue. This herb has been shown to reduce the occurrence and acuteness of colds. Some even claim it can help with issues of male virility. Simmer 1 teaspoon, either dried or fresh, in 1 cup (240 ml) freshly boiled water for 8–10 minutes three times a day.

Hibiscus (*Hibiscus sabdariffa*)

Beloved for the heavenly sweet perfume of the flowers, hibiscus is also a powerful diuretic and can lower blood pressure. As if that is not enough, it can also help sore throats and colds. Similar to other herbal applications, steep a tablespoon of the dried flowers in 1 cup (240 ml) freshly boiled water for 10 minutes and drink twice a day.

Kava (*Piper methysticum*)

This root is said to be highly effective as a muscle relaxer and for reducing anxiety. Kava can be handled the same as ginger, with 1 tablespoon of minced root or dried root taken as tea.

I recommend seeing how it affects you before you raise the dose to the recommended amounts of 2 or 3 cups of tea per day.

Licorice (*Glycyrrhiza glabra*)

This revered candy classic is also a wonderful anti-inflammatory which relieves the discomfort of colds in the sinuses. It can ease sore throats and coughs, and is also a tummy soother that is good for gut health. Use licorice root as you would ginger, with 1 minced teaspoon of fresh or dried root steeped in 1 cup (240 ml) freshly boiled water twice a day.

Marsh mallow (*Althaea officinalis*)

While it may seem like this is another "candy as medicine," marsh mallow is a time-tested plant long employed in field medicine. It is greatly valued as it contains a high amount of mucilage, which contains many beneficial antioxidants. Minced fresh or dried root or the leaves are equally healing. Use ¼ cup (10 g) in 1 cup (240 ml) water, steeped for 4 hours. Strain out the stems and drink hot or cool, sweetened or unsweetened—however you like this gentle herb.

Milk thistle (*Silybum marianum*)

Healers love milk thistle for its ability to protect the liver from toxins, harsh medicines, alcohol, and unseen environmental pollutants. It can be obtained as an extract at any health food store or upscale grocery or pharmacy. There is some evidence it can also help improve kidney conditions.

Look to the natural world to heal your mind, body, and soul.

Mullein (*Verbascum thapsus*)

Here is an herbalist's favorite for healing any respiratory ailment involving congestion, coughs, and sore throats, that can also calm the breathing. Mullein flowers infused in oil are also used to aid earaches. Steep one heaping tablespoon of the leaves in 1 cup (240 ml) boiling water for no more than 10 minutes. After one cup of tea, you'll feel better soon.

Nettle (*Urtica dioica*)

Nettle has been used as a healer for untold centuries and it relieves allergies, boosts the immune system, and can even help with a distended prostate. It is also a superfood and beloved for its nutrients. If you are working with fresh nettles, wear gloves to avoid the stings. Cooking or drying removes any irritant. Any herb or health food store will have dried nettle or nettles in a capsule form. Make nettle tea by steeping 2 teaspoons of leaves in 1 cup (240 ml) freshly boiled water for 10 minutes, or take the capsules in recommended doses of 300–500 mg twice a day.

GETTING HYGGE WITH YOUR HONEY

We might call it kitchen witchery and our Scandinavian friends could say it is how we "get hygge," which means to get as cozy as humanly possible. This newly trendy lifestyle tradition from the frozen north is not just for lazing about, though we greatly appreciate that aspect; it is also a very healthy way of living that includes lots of herbal food and drink, shared with your sweetheart, which is an immunity booster on its own. Tea is always a mainstay. For an ambrosial brew you can enjoy together, add a sliver of ginger root and a pinch each of echinacea and mint to a cup of hot black tea. Add a teaspoon of honey—then relax and enjoy together!

BLESSING BAG: YOUR HERBAL GOOD LUCK CHARM

Many plants have inherent magic that creates abundance, good fortune, and great luck. Harvest these herbs and create a blessing bag, which will allow you to harness their powers in your own backyard.

Gather together

Small muslin pouch with drawstring

1 teaspoon basil

1 teaspoon pine needles

1 teaspoon ground nutmeg

1 teaspoon rosemary

Fennel seed pod

Vanilla bean pod

3 cinnamon sticks, broken into pieces

Take the pouch and stuff it with the herbs. Add the fennel seed and vanilla bean pod and, lastly, the cinnamon sticks. Tie up the bag and, holding it in both hands, speak the following spell:

I hold in my hands these herbs of providence.

I hold in my heart, these herbs of destiny.

Blessings to all for the good of all.

And so it is. So mote it be.

Tie the bag to the back door of your home or wherever is closest to your plantings. Every time the door opens or closes, the little bag will deliver more good luck.

EASY PLANT MAGIC

I am lucky indeed to have had Aunt Edith, who was a gardener and herbalist. She had the greenest of thumbs and taught me everything I know about gardening. She was very patient and kindly taught me which wild plants were safe to eat and which sign of the moon was best for certain plants, as well as when to use this esoteric, albeit irresistible and fascinating, knowledge in magical workings. With her encouragement I developed my knowledge of how to make the most of the herbs, nuts, and flowers in the garden and the kitchen cupboard. Here are just a few quick fixes for instant results.

Acorns: A dried acorn is an excellent natural amulet for keeping a youthful appearance.

Alfalfa: Put a stalk in a small jar in the cupboard or pantry to ward off poverty.

Allspice: Burn ground allspice to attract luck and fortune, or use in herbal baths for healing.

Almond: Make offerings of almonds to the deities when you or loved ones need a speedy recovery.

Aloe: Grow in or around your home to prevent accidents or illness.

Bay leaf: Write a healing wish on a bay leaf and place it on your altar overnight.

Bayberry: Burn a white candle sprinkled with bayberry oil for good fortune and money.

Black cohosh: Use a cup of cool black cohosh tea as a hair rinse to restore your focus.

Carnation: Add 12 carnation flowers to your bath water for blooming health.

Chamomile: Tuck a chamomile teabag into your pillow for deep, sweet sleep.

Cumin: Add cumin to a goblet of wine for a spicy love spell.

Dandelion: Carry this herb in your pocket to bring luck in love and money.

Echinacea: Wash your hands in cool echinacea tea for greater physical strength.

Fennel: Both as a food ingredient and garden herb, fennel brings longevity.

Gardenia: In potpourri and as an essential oil, gardenia promotes peace of mind.

Ginseng: Carve a wish into a ginseng root and throw it into water to make the wish come true.

Hawthorn: An infusion of the herb used to wash floors will remove negative energies.

Honeysuckle: Crush the flowers and rub them into your forehead to enhance psychic powers.

Ivy: Encircle a yellow candle with ivy at the base and burn it for a day to repair a relationship.

Jasmine: Wear a crown of jasmine vine for prophetic visions and new ideas.

Lavender: Dried lavender flowers in a pouch under your pillow help heal depression.

Marjoram: Use an infusion in the bath for seven days to aid in resolving sadness or grief.

Mint: Use dried mint leaves to stuff a green doll figure or healing yourself or a loved one.

Mullein: Burn mullein to banish bad vibrations and bring a quick halt to bad habits.

Parsley: Use parsley in spells to increase strength and vitality after surgery or illness.

Poppy: Place dried poppy seeds into a pouch under your pillow to cure insomnia.

Rose: Rose petals in a bath help bruises and sprains heal much more quickly.

Rosemary: Wash your hands with an infusion of rosemary before any healing rituals for purification.

Sage: Burning sage is essential for self-purification and very helpful for recovering from grief and loss because it shifts energy in a positive way.

Spearmint: A ritual bath made with a cup of crushed spearmint leaves helps the lungs.

Violet: This flower of peace can be used in serenity spells.

Chapter 6

ESSENCES OF WELLBEING:
Aromatherapy and Essential Oils for Soul-care

Through my aunt Edith, I learned the art of drying roots, flowers, and herbs, as well as distilling and how certain plant essences and oils had the power to heal, cheer, and soothe both skin and moods. I eventually figured out she was a suburban hedgewitch and it only made me love my aunt more. She made sure I read widely, studied hard, and kept learning, which I continue to do. Plant magic remains a cherished subject for me and I have devoted years to essential oils, these concentrated oils extracted from plants. I love that this ancient art, utilized by many people, from Egyptians to Native Americans, is now so trendy and easily available to everyone—including busy moms, witches on the go, and suburban gals who garden. I have gathered here the essential oils and carrier oils that have proved most successful in my spells and healing work over the years. This is a veritable bounty of oils and practices to greatly abet the overall wellbeing of you and your loved ones.

CURING CARRIER OILS

A carrier oil, also known as a base oil, is a vegetable or plant-based oil that is used to dilute essential oils without diminishing the effect of the essence, and ensure that essential oils used topically are comfortable on the skin. Each essential oil carries specific vibrations that hold much curative power and these base oils support them, and can additionally be a vessel for healing in themselves.

Almond oil
This comes from the almond tree and is one of the carrier oils that can blend seamlessly with any other oil. It corresponds with Mercury, brightens the mind and mood, and is wonderful as a topical healer.

Apricot kernel oil
Imbued with sweetness and a warm energy, this strength-giving essence is especially good for women, nurturing them at every age and stage of life. Apricot oil also protects love.

Coconut oil
This oil is very thick and emanates a splendid fragrance that is immediately heartening. It is an emollient that not only soothes and heals skin and minor abrasions, but also has the magical properties of cleansing and purifying. It is associated with the element of water.

Evening primrose oil
This oil speeds the healing of bruises and wounds, and is extremely good for women, including helping with labor and easing pregnancy discomforts.

Evening primrose abets clairvoyance and paranormal gifts. It will help you to see clearly.

Grape-seed oil
Packed with vitamin E, this is fantastic for applying oils to your skin. It also augments spiritual growth. This should be one of the oils that you turn to for anointing yourself or any statues of gods and goddesses before rituals.

Jojoba oil
This oil absorbs extremely well into the skin, supporting and blending with anything it is mixed with. It is also a remarkable anointing oil. Jojoba should be used in recipes and rituals that help to deal with depression and support perseverance in hardship.

Olive oil
Connected to the element of fire, this oil is imbued with warmth and comfort. It was named "liquid gold" by the ancient Greek poet Homer, and rightly so: the healing properties have been greatly valued for millennia, as have the benefits to women, even increasing

fertility. It is associated with vitality, money, success, and joyfulness.

Sesame oil
A simply marvelous oil for your skin, it is absorbed lightly and easily. It is very rich in vitamins E and B, and in minerals which include calcium, magnesium, and phosphorus. It is an excellent emollient, and makes for a very pleasing massage oil.

Sunflower oil
Permeated with the energy of our sun, this oil is powerful and life-giving. Use it when you desire rapid growth and amplification of positive energy. Sunflower oil brings wisdom and is a protector.

QUICK AND EASY AROMATHERAPY

Essential oils have aromatic molecules that pass through the blood–brain barrier. This has a direct effect on the parts of our brain that control our state of anxiety, stress, and sadness. Application of these helpful essential oils to alleviate most negative emotions and moods can be quick and simple.

Breathing in relief: Drop one or two drops of the oil into the palm of your hand and slowly breath in the scent.

Pulse points: Put two drops onto a cotton ball and gently touch it to your temples and wrists to unwind.

Diffuse tension: Diffusers are popular in homes and offices as they simply emanate serenity. For tranquility when you're on the move, a couple of drops on a scarf around your neck will ease your way.

Medicinal mist: Plug the drain in your shower and turn on the hot water, then add five drops of oil. Let it run for a few minutes, then hop in and breathe in deeply. It is relaxing and invigorating at the same time.

BREATHE EASIER
These classic oils are excellent options for simple aromatherapy.

- Peppermint
- Eucalyptus
- Bergamot
- Tea tree
- Rosemary
- Thyme
- Geranium

RITUAL OF DAWN

How you begin your day can often set the tone for not only the entire day but also for beyond that. Therefore, it is incumbent upon us all to start out right! If you are not an early riser by nature, get up just a half hour earlier than usual to instill enchantment into your morning.

Gather together

1 green candle

1 yellow candle

1 orange candle

Peppermint essential oil

1 sprig fresh peppermint

Small dish for the plant

Immediately after you rise, place the items on your altar and dress the candles with the peppermint oil. Touch each candle with the peppermint sprig for just a moment. Light the candles, pick up the sprig with your left hand, and hold it to your face so you can breathe in the fresh and elevating fragrance as you speak aloud:

This is a blessed day, bright with possibilities.

Healing starts with this new day.

My body, mind, and heart are ready

All good things are coming my way.

So mote it be.

Spend a few moments in contemplation and reflection and breathe in the essence of the mint plant and oils. Visualize good things happening to you and picture yourself brimming with energy and exuberance.

ROSY YOU: A RITE OF GODDESSHOOD

You embody the Goddess, as all women do. It is important to acknowledge your goddesshood regularly and honor the goddesses who bless us all. This potion will remind you of all you are and that your life is downright rosy.

Combine ingredients in the bowl and stir with your finger widdershins (counterclockwise), as you chant the following spell twice:

We all come from the Goddess

And she is me,

I honor and embody her

I am a daughter of the goddess

And she is me.

And so it is. Blessed be.

Disrobe, stand in your shower, and anoint yourself with the oil, starting with your shoulders and working your way down. Repeat the chant once more as you apply the anointing oil.

When the bowl is empty, set it aside and shower. Allow your skin to dry naturally. As you go about your day, exult in your goddesshood and see the divinity in all who cross your path.

Gather together

1 cup (240 ml) jojoba or apricot oil

6 drops rose essential oil

4 drops gardenia essential oil

Bowl

SPICE UP YOUR LIFE POSITIVITY POTION

If you wear yourself out during the working week, as so many of us do, rubbing a tiny bit of this energy oil on your pulse points will brighten both your mood and your day instantly.

Gather together

1 cup (240 ml) sesame oil

½ teaspoon ground clove

½ teaspoon ground cinnamon

½ teaspoon ground ginger

½ teaspoon ground black pepper

6 drops neroli essential oil

6 drops jasmine essential oil

6 drops black pepper essential oil

Sealable amber-colored jar

Magnetite crystal

Small mixing bowl and spoon

Pour the sesame oil into the mixing bowl and then add in all the spices. Stir, add the oils, and stir again. Transfer to the jar and seal. Place the piece of magnetite onto your altar and place the jar beside it. Magnetite crystal (also known as lodestone) draws power and energy to you. Leave the crystal and potion there for a full week, and then use the oil to re-energize yourself by rubbing on your pulse points as needed.

FIND YOUR CELESTIAL ESSENCE

Every plant corresponds with certain planetary energies. Synergize with your astrological chart by trying the essential oils that match your sun sign and your moon sign, perhaps even in combination, in your magical and healing workings. Have fun and keep notes in your Book of Shadows about what works for you.

Aries, ruled by Mars: carnation, cedar, clove, juniper, peppermint, and pine.

Taurus, ruled by Venus: apple, lilac, oak moss, orchid, plumeria, rose, vanilla, and violet.

Gemini, ruled by Mercury: almond, bergamot, peppermint, lavender, lemongrass, and lily.

Cancer, ruled by the Moon: eucalyptus, gardenia, jasmine, lemon, myrrh, and sandalwood.

Leo, ruled by the Sun: acacia, cinnamon, orange, and rosemary.

Virgo, ruled by Mercury: almond, bergamot, cypress, spearmint, and patchouli.

Libra, ruled by Venus: catnip, marjoram, mugwort, spearmint, sweet pea, and vanilla.

Scorpio, ruled by Pluto: allspice, basil, galangal, and ginger.

Sagittarius, ruled by Jupiter: anise, cedarwood, and honeysuckle.

Capricorn, ruled by Saturn: lemon thyme, mimosa, vervain, and vetiver.

Aquarius, ruled by Uranus: citron, cypress, lavender, pine, and spearmint.

Pisces, ruled by Neptune: neroli, orris, and sweet pea.

KEEPING YOU IN THE FULL BLOOM OF HEALTH

It is little wonder that many essential oils have been in use and relied upon for millennia as healers of body, mind, and spirit. They almost always have multi-uses, with excellent applications for physical wellbeing, for emotional and mental wellness, and to aid meditation in spiritual self-care.

Benzoin, bringer of blessings

This powerhouse will connect you more deeply to your soul and the realm of spirit. It is also a great comfort in times of trouble. In olden times it was used to ward off evil spirits and is still used for that purpose in some parts of the world. Benzoin oil protects us from the bad and brings many blessings.

Banish bad energy with black pepper

Derived from the common peppercorn, this oil promotes emotional wellness and relaxes the nervous system. Black pepper oil can be administered topically for stimulating the senses and engendering courage. It is also a protectant and can help keep bad energy and bad people out of your home.

Gentle healer gardenia

With a richly sweet floral scent that is calming, this oil is useful for much more than scented candles and perfumes—it is a power healer. Gardenia essential oil has major anti-inflammatory properties so it is an effective topical remedy for treating inflammatory issues, such as arthritis. It is also really helpful for improving gut health.

Lift your spirits with lavender

A truly versatile essential oil, this is a natural antibiotic, antiseptic, sedative, antidepressant, and topical treatment for scalds and burns, and a good detoxifier. Lavender promotes healing, and the lovely scent has a calming effect and is widely used in aromatherapy.

Narcissus to reach the next level

With roots in Greek mythology, this visionary essence takes you to the realm of imagination. If you want to have intense dreams to feed your creativity, narcissus can bring those to you. Use it in conjunction with more grounding essential oils, so you also attend to practical matters as you explore.

Nutmeg for new luck and love

This is a warm, spicy essential oil that is sweet and somewhat woody. It blends beautifully with other essential oils in the spice family and strengthens the combination. Nutmeg is very lucky and is wonderful in money magic. It is also fortunate for romance and instills loyalty in a relationship.

Transform energy with tea tree

Used by Aboriginal people in Australia for centuries, this oil has powerful antibacterial, antifungal, and antiseptic properties. It has a fresh camphor smell and is used for space clearing and energy management. It can rid your home of negative energy swiftly and be used to ward off malevolent spirits. Use tea tree essential oil to clear out and reset vibrations after an illness.

Vanilla, essence of contentment

Obtained from the bean of the same name, vanilla has one of the most comforting, heartening, and sweet scents of all. It is very useful for cheering up yourself or anyone else who needs it. It is excellent for house magic to create a cozy and safe sanctuary and also very useful in spellwork for love and romance. It raises your personal energy level and is good for imbuing your home with positive, pleasant energy. Vanilla also helps with mental focus.

Ylang-ylang for love

This richly perfumed essential oil is a mood-booster, anti-inflammatory, and aphrodisiac, benefitting both the mind and body. Ylang-ylang instills confidence, overcomes shyness, and is exceptional when used for sensual spells and love charms.

PAIN-RELIEVING POTIONS

More folks are flocking to essential oils for their medicinal properties as topicals. The combination of the remedial herbaceous scents in steams and mists for coughs, colds, and headaches and as rubs for achy joints and sore muscles is unmatched— and also healthy for the budget. Best of all, they're completely natural.

Rosemary

This woody and sweet-smelling oil is a healer for flu, coughs, headaches, depression, muscular stress, arthritis, rheumatism, fatigue, and forgetfulness. Rosemary essential oil is stimulating and will perk you up if you do a head steam. You can also put a couple of drops in the bath to help aches, pains, and sniffles go away. It is unusual in that it can both relax you and stimulate your mind. Rosemary has a very cleansing energy and can imbue your home with coziness and contentment.

Thyme

This "old-time" curative was highly valued and widely used by the ancient Egyptians, Greeks, and Romans and was beloved by hedgewitch healers. It can lessen pain and quicken recovery. It confers boldness, and is also a restorative to anyone who has faced challenges or great loss. It is a favorite in green witchery and house magic as a protectant.

Bay

The soothing essence extracted from bay laurel leaves has magical properties for both physical and mental healing. With an herbaceous scent, bay essential oil is the perfect choice for relieving migraines and sore muscles. It is also invaluable for psychic development, removing hexes, and any type of attraction magic.

Frankincense

An ancient essence that has long been considered precious, this earthy and woody oil is perfect for clearing blocked nasal passageways to promote better breathing. Native to regions of northern Africa, this oil's benefits can be obtained by inhaling or massaging pressure points with it for relief of aches, soreness, and sprains. It is prized for use in magical workings and highest rituals. Plus, it keeps evil away.

Comfrey

Beloved by healers, comfrey is one of the best-known healing herbs of all times. In ancient times, comfrey leaves were placed over wounds and even broken bones so they would knit together. It has even been referred to as "a one-herb pharmacy" for its inherent curative powers. Well-known and widely used by early Greeks and Romans, its very name, *symphytum*, from the Greek *symphyo* which means to "make grow together," refers to its traditional use of healing fractures. Comfrey essential oil has a strong protective energy and can also prevent you from losing both love and money.

HEADACHE HELPERS: ESSENTIAL OILS THAT ALLEVIATE DISCOMFORT

• Palo Santo essential oil is a resinous, richly-scented essence that offers the benefits of protection and purification and for this reason it has been used by Native Americans and shamans for millennia. They use it to connect to the divine. It is also very good for abetting breath, overcoming headaches, and lifting depression. It is commonly utilized in aromatherapy and in soothing massages. Opt for Palo Santo when you need to replace negative energy with positive.

• Yarrow essential oil is good for both body and mind and can help with anxiety, tension headaches, muscle aches, and overall mental wellness. It has a cooling effect on emotions and muscles. A very pretty plant, flowering stalks of yarrow can be bundled together and hung on front doors to ward off any evil, including people. The oil brings courage, will make you lucky in love, and can heal a broken heart or spirit.

• Mugwort has long been used in magical workings, first in Mesopotamia and then expanding throughout Europe, Asia, and now the rest of the world. It is used by seers and shamans for achieving new levels of consciousness. Mugwort essential oil is especially good for the mental plane: it helps overcome headaches and soothes anxiety for mental balance and calm. It will help you hone your psychic abilities (see page 11), which will help and guide you on your journey of life.

SKIN-SOOTHING SOLUTIONS

Not only helpful for the mind, essential oils can also be extremely beneficial for the body. These are your go-to-glow oils for your home spa.

Carrot seed

This warm and deeply comforting oil soothes the soul by keeping anxiety and stress at bay. Carrot seed essential oil has antimicrobial, antioxidant, and anti-inflammatory properties, making it a great anti-aging agent for aging skin. Carrot seed enhances empathy, is pleasingly grounding, and removes spiritual blocks.

Eucalyptus

This essential oil comes from the leaves of the eucalyptus plant, native to Australia. Fresh and minty, eucalyptus essential oil carries medicinal, antiseptic, and pharmaceutical benefits. It is wonderful for the skin and not only abets healing but also can bring back a youthful glow. These powerful properties are most often released by adding a few drops of this oil into water. In eucalyptus oil, we have an all-purpose therapeutic for coughs, colds, respiratory stimulation, and insect bites. If you start to feel cold symptoms, use five drops of eucalyptus oil in a hot bath or in a bowl filled with boiling water for a head steam.

Myrrh

This precious essential essence from pre-Biblical times is prized for its warm and lightly musk-smelling oil. Hailed for its considerable anti-inflammatory properties, it is great for reducing pain and calming blotchy skin. An excellent anointing oil for candles, lamps, and also for yourself, this essential oil will connect you to the sacred dimension.

Palmarosa

Also referred to as Indian Geranium, this is a sweetly-scented essential oil with a hint of lemon and rose. It contains great benefits used topically on skin, being both smoothing and soothing. It also mends a broken heart and can be used in heart-healing spells. Palmarosa will connect you to a higher vibration and angelic energy.

Peppermint

A wonderful therapeutic for headaches, skin irritations, and depression, it is not surprising that peppermint essential oil is regarded as one of the world's oldest medicines. It is first rate in money magic and healing work, and also can be useful in divination.

RESTORATION RITE

This rite imbues a handmade massage oil with healing power, created by setting an intention to help a loved one who is unwell or in pain.

Pour the base oils into the double-boiler pan and warm them very slowly over a low heat. Stir the oils gently until they are combined, then add the essential oils to the mixture. Stir slowly and gently and intone:

Our bodies can heal.

Our bodies come from this earth.

This essence of healing comes from the earth,

Fed by the sun, fed by the rain.

By my hands, this healing is begun.

So mote it be.

Carefully pour the warm, but not hot, oils into the clay bowl. Pour a palmful into your hand and begin soothingly massaging your loved one's shoulders and back with the mixture. In addition to the healing properties of the oils themselves, the smell of the combination is incredibly uplifting and will remind you both of a brilliantly sunny day at the ocean on a sandy beach. In this way, it is doubly healing. The anise oil adds a light tingling sensation which awakens the senses and invigorates the skin and the muscles being rubbed. Triple healing!

Gather together:

½ cup (120 ml) coconut oil

½ cup (120 ml) almond oil

Double-boiler pan

15 drops comfrey essential oil

10 drops bergamot essential oil

8 drops anise essential oil

Clay bowl and wooden spoon

PRIMROSE PATH WELLBEING BALM

All essential oils can be turned into balms and salves by adding beeswax. Making your own remedies at home can be most rewarding as it is part of the practice of self-healing. This balm has myriad healing properties and can help with scratches, bruises, and sore muscles, along with emotional upsets and blue moods. With this handy recipe, you will be on the path to wellbeing. This recipe can be easily adapted to make other balms, such as bay leaf balm or lavender and calendula balm, both favorites of mine. Experimentation is an important part of your wellness journey!

Gather together

10 drops grapeseed oil

10 drops palmarosa essential oil

10 drops lavender essential oil

10 drops evening primrose oil

6 drops tea tree essential oil

4 tablespoons (55 g) beeswax

Double-boiler pan

Mixing bowl and wooden spoon

Sealable pint (560-ml) jar or lidded tin

Combine the grapeseed oil and all the essential oils in the mixing bowl. Transfer the oils to the double-boiler pan and add the beeswax. Slowly heat until the wax is fully melted. Stir gently with the wooden spoon, then pour the mixture into a clean, dry jar. Seal the jar and label it with the ingredients and date. Store it in a cupboard away from sunlight and heat and use within 6 months. This sublimely soothing balm will be there at your beck and call.

CALM CONTENTMENT

We have all come to know and love certain essential oils, such as lavender, clary sage, chamomile, ylang ylang, comfrey, and jasmine, for their widely known stress-reducing properties. However, there are several others that were relied upon by hedgewitches and the ancients for their therapeutic and recuperative properties.

Bergamot
This oil's origins can be traced to Southeast Asia, where it was prized for its spicy and floral scent. Bergamot essential oil is most often used to lift moods and alleviate stress. Send anxiety packing with bergamot essential oil; bergamot is like liquid sunshine. It is exceptional for house magic.

Cypress
Originating from the eastern Mediterranean region, this mystical oil soothes the soul and is a balm for those who are suffering grief, despair, and hopelessness. With an evergreen and lightly spicy aroma, cypress oil can connect you in a positive way to loved ones who have passed on. Cypress offers strength, more energy, and new hope.

Hyssop
Native to the Mediterranean region, this oil is rich in spiritual properties. With a minty smell, it can be used to purify and abet the release of grief, sadness, and depression. It is a protective oil that can be used for clearing away negative energy after an upset or from your home environment.

Sage
Gaining popularity in the Middle Ages, this spicy oil contains natural antidepressants and antibacterial and stress reduction properties. It is used in aromatherapy to reduce the user's anxiety and clarify their conscience.

Spikenard
This is a wonderful tried-and-true stress reducer. With an earthy and woody aroma, this oil is great for calming its user spiritually and can even alleviate insomnia. Perhaps the finest quality of spikenard essential oil is that it will help you forgive, let go, and make peace with anyone who has hurt you, clearing the way for a fresh start and new beginnings.

Tarragon
With a tangy aroma, this is a great agent to overcome worry, upset, and a negative frame of mind. Tarragon oil can be used to heal after a shock and helps with the resulting trauma. This oil is a protectant, bringing strength and recovery from deep distress. It can also aid a restful night's sleep.

DIVINE FEMININE BLEND

This anointing oil can be used as an altar offering to goddesses by dressing candles with it, as well as adorning and honoring yourself. It will deepen your connection to the divine feminine and also is an act of sacred self-care. It will help you appear ageless, and is superb for your skin. After all, you are divine, too.

Gather together

6 tablespoons (90 ml) sunflower seed oil

6 tablespoons (90 ml) sweet almond oil

2 drops pomegranate seed essential oil

2 drops neroli essential oil

2 drops myrrh essential oil

2 drops carrot seed essential oil

Small mixing bowl and spoon

Small sealable jar

Pour all the oils into the bowl, starting with the sunflower seed and sweet almond oils and adding in each essential oil by the dropper. Stir nine times, then carefully transfer the oils to the sealable jar. Place the jar on your altar and leave it there for an entire 24 hours before using.

At night, anoint your skin with the oil, intoning this spell:

Mother of us all, hear this prayer.

May I be a reflection of you.

May I reflect all that is right and true.

Goddess of light—hear this prayer.

Blessings to all; blessed be me.

Pour three drops of the oil into your palm and gently touch the potion to your face. Smooth it into your skin, being careful to avoid your eye area. Using warm water, rinse off for a goddess-like glow.

Repeat this ritual each night, and keep the oil on your altar for future offerings to the Goddess.

DIVINITY DISTILLATIONS

These wise woman oils are sacred to the Goddess.

• Myrtle: This slightly sweet and camphor scented essential oil is pressed from the eucalyptus plant, which was dedicated to Aphrodite in Ancient Greece. It can balance energies, increase mood quality, prevent allergies, and clarify and cleanse emotional blockages. Myrtle is marvelous for use in goddess rites.

• Pomegranate seed: This essential oil gives powers of divination, makes wishes come true, and engenders wealth. Carry a muslin or cotton sachet anointed with this oil for luck. Associated with the Goddess and divine daughterhood, it is also an important anointing oil for new witches or women entering maidenhood and cronehood.

• Oakmoss: With an earthy energy to match the name, this oil can ground you and remind you of what you are supposed to accomplish during your life. It is very uplifting and brings inspiration.

Oakmoss essential oil is an attractor of abundance and highly recommended for money spells. It is also associated with older women, and any rituals of cronehood and elder woman's wisdom should include oakmoss oil.

• Neroli oil: Extracted from the bitter orange tree, originally found in Egypt, Algeria, France, and Spain, this essence contains regenerative qualities, making it perfect for topical applications to alleviate upset skin and reduce redness. It is a goddess oil with a gentle feminine energy that both lifts emotions and helps overcome fear and worry. It can be used to receive messages from dreams, as well as for astral travel.

DEEP REST AND SWEET DREAMS

Many of us suffer from insomnia. The following essential oils can bring peaceful sleep.

Agrimony

Used since ancient times, this oil is very highly regarded as an all-purpose healer for the body. Turn to agrimony for help with sleep. It is a protective herb which brings about a sense of wellbeing and ease. Remember agrimony oil for your wellness rituals.

Anise

This carries a strong scent of licorice and has a wide variety of usages. It is excellent for renewed vitality, and can be applied topically in combination with carrier oils for therapeutic massage. It also makes for deep, peaceful sleep and protects against nightmares.

Caraway

This oil enables us to rise above the earthly plane and see life in spiritual terms. It strengthens mental alertness and enhances memory. Caraway essential oil will protect your aura and empower visionary dreams if you sprinkle a couple of drops on your pillowcase at night before sleep.

Mimosa

This oil will help you relax and can even bring deep, dream-filled sleep. Mimosa has a lightly honeyed scent and has a very important aspect in that it will abet self-esteem and self-love. It will draw positive love toward you in spellwork. Try mimosa in a steam bath or as a perfume you wear to imbue and surround yourself with a sense of self-worth.

Rosewood

Great for easing its user into a restful night's sleep, this oil can be used to calm restlessness and overcome the blues. It has a very balancing energy, can aid burnout, helps with renewal, and brings a youthful feeling.

Spruce

Sometimes referred to as Black Spruce, this woody and rich oil can promote mental clarity for its user. It is also very grounding for when you feel scattered. It was long used as a medicinal by Native Americans who valued the positive effects to mind, body, and spirit. Smelling the scent in a mist or diffuser can aid breathing, relax you, and help you sleep. You can also use it for purification rituals, as did the Native Americans.

Valerian

Originally from Europe and Asia, this oil engenders an overall feeling of relaxation in its user. It can be used to deter restlessness, promote a full night's rest, and is a great and nurturing aroma for girls and women. Valerian is also an anointing oil and is said to bring luck to your endeavors. It was especially popular during medieval times, when it was regarded as a major healing herb for many maladies.

SWEET SLEEP SPELL

If you have slept poorly recently, reset with this simple and useful spell.

Right before you get into bed, place the lavender stalks into the bag. Take the blue ribbon and anoint it with rosewood oil seven times. Tie the muslin bag with the ribbon. Hold the bag in both hands and crush it slightly, so the lavender releases its tranquil fragrance. Then speak aloud:

On this and every night,

Deep rest is within sight.

Each morning, I will awaken to light

Each day, my energy is fresh and bright.

And so it is; so mote it be.

Place the muslin bag under your pillow and you will sleep deeply and awaken refreshed and restored.

Gather together

7 dried lavender stalks

Small muslin bag

7-inch (18-cm) piece of dark blue ribbon

Rosewood essential oil

Chapter 7

SACRED SELF-CARE STONES: Crystals, Gems, and Geodes

The earliest humans made use of the unique properties of crystals. For example, amber, one of my absolute favorite gems, was probably the first stone used as ornamentation, when people of the Stone Age discovered rock-hard resin deposits. Roughly rounded beads were used for necklaces, belts, and pouches. Archeologists and anthropologists have found many sites in which precious amber was buried with the tools and remains of shamans, medicine men, and rulers. Since the beginning of mankind, this stone has been thought to have healing properties, a belief that stays with us to this day. But the Egyptians were perhaps the people most conscious of the power of crystals, using them even in the cornerstones of the Great Pyramids. They used gems as objects of protection, power, wisdom, and love for both the living and the dead. Secret knowledge of these sacred stones and their magical properties has been passed down to us and it has been embraced very enthusiastically. This is wonderful as it is one more way Mother Earth offers her healing energy.

CRYSTAL CLEANSING SALT SPELL

The first thing you need to do when you get a new crystal is to cleanse it, so it does not shed any potentially negative vibrations from others. This can be done with a simple salt ritual.

Gather together

1 cup (200 g) sea salt

Glass bowl

Crystal to be cleansed

Black candle

Sage bundle

Fireproof dish

Add the salt to the glass bowl and put your crystal on top of the salt. Light the black candle, then light the sage from the candle flame and put it in the fireproof dish. Speak this spell:

Bone of the earth, filled with ancient power,

Filled with grounding, filled with healing.

Let go of all that came before.

You are now here.

You are welcome here.

With harm to none, and blessings to all.

Roll the crystal so every side touches the salt and then repeat the spell. Snuff both the sage and the candle and let the stone rest in the salt overnight. In the morning, remove the crystal and let it power up on your altar to become imbued with your energy and magical intention. Take the salt out of your home and dispose of it at least a block away. Your stone is now ready to serve your needs.

ELIXIR OF ENCHANTMENT

Adding a tiny crystal to potions harnesses the energy of the crystal. Amethyst is a calming crystal that will add serenity to your space in a home mister.

Fill the bottle three quarters full with the distilled water. Drop in the tiny crystal so it floats down to the bottom of the bottle. Add the neroli and vanilla essential oils and seal the bottle. Shake it gently. Before spraying around your home, chant aloud:

This is a home of peace.

This is a home of happiness.

Happiness lives here.

Healthiness lives here.

And so it is.

Gather together

1-fluid ounce (30-ml) blue spray bottle

Distilled water

Small amethyst crystal

3 drops vanilla essential oil

3 drops neroli essential oil

WORRY-FREE STONES

Humans have been using worry stones for millennia and even certain rosary beads serve that function. Living in our modern age, we need to take that concept to the next level with worry-free wellbeing stones.

Take a small muslin bag or pouch in a fabric you love, and add at least two small polished pebbles of the following crystals:
- amber for joyfulness
- turquoise for grounded calm
- onyx for protection
- tiger's eye to fend off psychic vampires
- pink jade for self-compassion
- lepidolite for letting go of care and worry.

CHAKRA HEALING CRYSTALS

The chakras are energy hotspots on the body. Crystals can help channel positive energy into them and encourage the release of negative energy through them.

Cuprite

This mineral crystal is formed from copper ore and can have needle-like crystals of a brilliant red inside a nearly black crystal. It has a spectacular sparkle. In the same way that copper has wonderful health benefits (see page 125), so does cuprite, helping with concerns in the heart, blood, skin, muscles, and bones. Cuprite stimulates the lower chakra. It is a handy stone to take on air flights, as it can treat altitude sickness. It also furthers the functions of the bladder and kidneys.

Dioptase

This gorgeous gemstone is nearly the color of emerald but lacks the hardness, thus lowering its marketplace value. The true value of dioptase lies in its ability to help anyone experiencing mental stress. It lends balance to male and female energies and acts as a stabilizer. As an energy stone, dioptase can activate and awaken all of the chakras. When you wear dioptase, you will fascinate admirers with this beautiful stone and find peace of mind in the process.

Selenite

This chakra healer helps rid unhealthy and negative thoughts, yours or others', from your mind and etheric body. It is a record-keeping stone and carries information from the centuries on Earth it has witnessed. It can also be placed over the third eye to access stored information about your past lives. In the same way this crystal retains, it is good for letting go and helps you forgive. Selenite can also be used for healing of the nerves, reproductive organs, and spine, lending flexibility. With its white swirls, selenite can give an enormous boost to creative visualization, and can be a most auspicious crystal ball for gazing. A rare kind of selenite is gold selenite from Australia, which is good for grounding.

Sugilite

Another forgiveness and letting-go stone, sugilite is so powerful that it can help with channeling. Placed on the third-eye area, it alleviates sadness and despondency, and protects your very soul from the frustration and disillusionment of this world. This healing stone dispels headaches and gently draws pain out of afflicted areas, bringing respite to inflammations, toxicity, and stress-related illness. Sugilite has been used to great effect to ease the discomfort of those suffering from cancer. This stone also absorbs anger, hurt, and energies that you have unwittingly picked up and are draining you. If you have problems with jealousy, it helps you rise above any pettiness and bring out your best side. I love that sugilite creates a sense of belonging for those who always felt like outsiders.

Turquoise

This opens the heart chakra and also affords a heart-centered quality, a loving connection with others. Turquoise releases negative emotions and draws out unsettling vibrations. After using turquoise as a "drawing stone," place it on the ground afterward, because the earth can absorb and process the negativity that is no longer inside you. Turquoise will help you find your deepest, truest self: it inspires and uplifts, offering elevation to the chakras. The properties of this stone are as practical as they are spiritual—igniting intuition and enabling the wearer to grow toward wholeness. As a healer, turquoise can be placed gently upon an area of affliction for quick pain relief. It is especially helpful for headaches.

THE SEVEN CHAKRAS

- Crown chakra—at the top of your head
- Third-eye chakra—in the center of your forehead
- Throat chakra—in the center of your throat
- Heart chakra—in the center of your chest
- Solar plexus chakra—at the bottom of the breastbone
- Sacral chakra—just below the navel
- Root chakra—at the base of the spine

ROCKS THAT RESTORE THE BODY

The simplest way to access healing with crystal is to wear a stone. While you are enjoying the considerable benefits to your wellbeing conferred by crystals, you can also appreciate the unmatched beauty provided by Mother Nature herself.

Brightening albite

Albite is the sister of the polished moonstone. A milky-colored stone with blue shading, it can be found in Africa, Europe, and the Americas. Albite is helpful for the immune system and breathing problems, and can assist the spleen and thyroid. This translucent stone calms the wearer and fights depression. A chunk of albite in your bedroom will help banish the blues.

Amazing amethyst

Amethyst is one of the stones most esteemed by healers. The legendary American psychic Edgar Cayce recommended it for control and temperance. Amethyst is believed to aid in the production of hormones and regulate the circulatory, immune, and metabolic systems. It is treasured for its centering and calming properties and seems to connect directly to the mind, fighting emotional swings and depression. Aquarians and Pisceans can count it as their birthstone, and this might be a very good thing because the Fishes frequently struggle with substance-abuse issues, and amethyst can conquer drinking and other sensory indulgences, such as out-of-control sexuality. Amethyst also helps with mental focus, intuition, meditation, and memory.

Awesome aventurine

Aventurine is one of those rare general healers that can offer wellness to any part of the body upon which it is laid. As a general healing stone, it can also be used in tandem with other stones, such as rose quartz and malachite. Combined with rose quartz, aventurine can help open your heart and soul to love and compassion. Used in combination with malachite, the benefits are clarity and raised consciousness. Highly recommended and an excellent boon for young children, aventurine is a wonder stone for the wellbeing of the whole family.

Boosting bloodstone

Bloodstone is a recent name for this powerful restorative. The ancient name for this variegated chalcedony quartz is "heliotrope." It stands to reason that bloodstone would be connected with blood and the circulatory system. It is also used to detoxify the liver, kidneys, and spleen. In India, bloodstone is ground up and taken in an elixir as an aphrodisiac. A belief stemming from ancient times is that bloodstone can give great courage and help avoid harmful situations. All in all, bloodstone enriches the blood, calms the mind, and increases the consciousness of the wearer. This is a great gem for you if you have a sedentary and detail-oriented job.

Astonishing Botswana agate

Botswana agate is named for the region in which it is found, and is gray in color, looking smooth and waxy. Botswana agate is good for the skin, the lungs, and the respiratory system—making it a powerful tool for anyone dealing with smoke, whether a firefighter or a smoker who wants to quit the habit. It can also boost moods and help fight depression.

Calming calcite

Calcite is helpful to bones and joints and is a memory booster. In addition to aiding the retention of information, calcite is a calming agent that can bring clarity to decision-making processes. Green calcite is a terrific support to people in transition, bringing about positive energy in place of the negative. The yellow and gold calcites are useful for meditation thanks to their association with the sun, light, the sign of the spiritual path, and higher knowledge. It is said that these sunny calcites can even help with astral projection. Calcite is a healing stone and is highly recommended for physicians, nurses, and healers to keep at their offices.

Chakra-enhancing carnelian

Carnelian is linked with the lower chakras, can heal holes in the etheric body, and can give support for letting go of anger, old resentments, and emotions that no longer serve a positive purpose. Orange carnelian is especially beloved for its ability to promote energy and vitality by warming the emotions. If worn at your throat, carnelian overcomes timidity and lends the power of great and eloquent speech. Like some other red stones, it also gives you courage. In addition, wearing carnelian can offer you a sense of comfort and create the proper atmosphere for meditation and total clarity of mind and thought. Carnelian as a pendant or on a belt gives you control of your thoughts and understanding of others.

Curative chrysocolla

Chrysocolla is a stone associated with Gaia, our Earth Mother, and also Kwan Yin, the benevolent bringer of compassion. Chrysocolla evokes the qualities of these goddesses: nurture, forgiveness, and tolerance. It is viewed as a lunar stone, perfect for meditations with the new moon and on global issues such as the environment and world peace. By merely holding this placid piece of earth in your hand, you can send healing energy out to the planet.

Medicinal moss agate

Moss agate is usually a dark color: brown, black, or blue. Moss agate comes from India, North America, or Australia. It is named as such because it has patterning in light-colored clusters that resembles moss. This is a cleansing stone and can bring balance to both sides of the brain, therefore reducing depression or emotional ailments. Moss agate is also useful for treating hypoglycemia. It is the stone of farmers, botanists, and midwives—those who nurture new life. It also aids intuition and creativity and can reduce inhibition and shyness, so it is great to wear if you are a speaker, singer, or performer.

Releasing rhodonite

Rhodonite aligns the physical, emotional, and mental facets of your entire being and brings balance to them. If you are feeling ungrounded and scattered, this crystal will soothe and uplift. This confidence crystal can help you attain your greatest potential. The highest-grade gem form of rhodonite awakens the intuition. As a healer, rhodonite alleviates the shock that accompanies a grievous loss. It is also used for issues involving the ears and hearing and is said to be very good for bone growth. Rhodonite helps build a healthy emotional foundation, and I think the best and highest use of rhodonite is for healing old emotional wounds and scars, letting you grow from the experience. If you are feeling low-grade anxiety, this is an excellent crystal to carry in your pocket as a touchstone.

HEALING CRYSTAL RINGS

• Malachite is best used as a ring on your right hand to prevent burnout and restore you.

• Wear opal on your right hand and your wellness wishes will be granted!

• Wear onyx only on your left hand for relieving stress and quieting the mind.

• Moonstone boosts your self-regard and optimism if worn in a ring with a silver setting.

• Red garnet overcomes lethargy and engenders a new lease on life.

• Jasper rings help heal the skin and maintain a youthful appearance.

• Citrine helps with stomach aches and mental clarity, and increases powers of concentration.

• Pearls are very soothing and will calm headaches and uplift you.

SOUL-HEALING STONES

Crystals have the power not only to perform physical healing but also to care for our emotions.

Labradorite

Labradorite is a bluish feldspar soul stone with a very powerful light-energy. It abets astral travel, the higher mind, and intelligence and is a favorite of mystics. It brings up nothing but the positive for the brain and consciousness and excises the lower energies of anxiety, stress, and negative thoughts. It is an aura cleanser and balancer. Labradorite, which used to be called spectrolite, also protects against aura leakage. This is a crystal to hold and keep with you during meditation for psychic flashes, much like the flashes of light from within the stone.

Malachite

Malachite can help restore anyone who is suffering from burnout. Those who do psychic work and healing are among those who are affected by this most severely, so they need to keep malachite nearby for rejuvenation. Malachite opens the heart and throat chakras and rebalances the solar plexus, enabling realignment of the psychic and etheric bodies.

Rose quartz

Rose quartz engenders self-love, which we must have before we can really love anyone else. Self-forgiveness and self-acceptance are made possible with rose quartz meditation. I keep a very large piece of rose quartz with a light centered at the base of my bed, and the warm pink glow immediately makes the room a comforting cocoon. The heat of the bulb also causes the stone to release cheery negative ions into my bedroom. Rose quartz is a crystal of tenderness, nurturing, compassion, sympathy, and faith. This rock has healing power over the heart and the circulatory system, as well as the reproductive and cleansing organs. Traditionally, rose quartz is believed to abet fertility. It is especially good for sensitive souls—artists, writers, musicians, poets, and anyone of a gentle and receptive nature. Quartz is the largest of the crystal families, and we can be grateful for that since it is such a powerful healer. Moreover, it is an energy regulator for the human body, affecting the vibrations of the aura (the energy field that surrounds all living beings).

ASTRAL AZURITE SPELL

The great psychic and healer Edgar Cayce used this blue beauty for achieving remarkable meditative states during which he had astoundingly accurate visions and prophetic dreams. Indeed, azurite helps achieve a high state of mental clarity and powers of concentration. If you cannot find the answer to a problem in the here and now, try looking for solutions on the astral plane.

First, write the problem down on paper and place it under a small azurite overnight on a windowsill so it collects moonlight.

The next day at 11:11 a.m., lie comfortably in a quiet and darkened room with the azurite stone placed over your third eye (between your eyebrows) on your forehead. Clear your mind of everything for 11 minutes and meditate. Sit up and listen for the first thing that comes into your mind—it should be the answer or a message regarding the issue at hand. Write down the words you receive. The rest of the day you will be in a state of grace and higher mind, during which you will hear information and answers to help guide you in many aspects of your life.

If, like me, you enjoy this meditation, you may want to do it every day at 11:11 a.m. and every night at 11:11 p.m. I strongly suggest that you keep a journal of these "azurite answers." You may receive information that you will not understand until many years have passed, making the journal an invaluable resource and key to your very special life.

SECRET GEM REMEDIES: A WEEK OF WELLNESS

Gemstones and crystals have healing powers based on ancient belief systems. The secrets below come to us from the Chaldeans, who were master astrologers with advanced knowledge of the sun, stars, and our earth, and reveal how to amplify a crystal's power by working with it on a specific day.

Monday: Pearl

Pearls radiate orange rays and operate as a curative if worn on Mondays, starting first thing in the morning. They help with mental wellness, diabetes, colic, and fever.

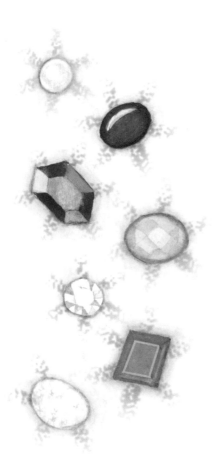

Tuesday: Ruby

Rubies on Tuesdays are a boon! Ruby heals the heart and carries the red ray of emotional wellness through the expression of love. This is divine energy, and as such there is a striving for the highest love vibration. Ruby brings joy into your life and gives you permission to follow your bliss.

Wednesday: Emerald

Emerald has green light rays and can help with the heart, ulcers, asthma, and influenza, when worn on Wednesday, starting two hours after dawn.

Thursday: Topaz

Topaz has blue rays and helps with laryngitis, arthritis, anxiety and upset, fever, and various glandular disorders if worn on Thursdays.

Friday: Diamond

Diamonds, containing rays of indigo light, are for eyes, nose, asthma, and laziness, and to prevent drunkenness, especially if worn on Friday. Wearing diamonds in conjunction with a waxing moon enhances their power.

Saturday: Sapphire

Sapphire has violet energy. Worn on Saturday on the middle finger of the right hand two hours before sunset, the stone is said to help the kidneys, epilepsy, and sciatica.

Sundays: Opal

Sundays are a holy day, when you will come into your soul's true purpose by wearing opal jewelry with its rainbow-colored rays.

THE HEALING POWER OF JADE

Jade is globally renowned as a blessing stone. Jade brings with it the power of health, wealth, love, and protection. It is also a dream stone, promoting prophetic and deeply meaningful dreams. There is an entire spectrum of jade and each color has its own beneficent properties.

Types of jade

- Purple jade heals the broken heart, allowing understanding and acceptance in and pain and anger out. If you are going through a breakup, purple jade will help you with the heartache.
- Green jade is a wisdom stone and can help relationships that aren't working become functional instead of dysfunctional. This shade is also a boon for the brain. Green jade helps with focus.

- Red jade promotes the proper release of anger and also generates healthy sensual passion.
- Blue jade brings patience and composure and is great for conveying a sense of safety and serenity.
- Yellow jade is excellent for energy, simple joy, and maintaining the sense of being a part of a greater whole.

MYSTICAL METALS

Just as the first ancients sensed that stones contained energy and special properties, they also discovered that metals hold energies of tremendous influence and power. Metals used to be very commonplace in magic, but their use waned during the late medieval era when alchemists began to become scientists. Metallurgy has rebounded and plays a definite role in the magic of jewelry.

Gold gives the power of the sun

Gold is aligned with our star, the sun, and is beloved for its sheen and purity. It is a fantastic energy conductor in its white, yellow, or rose form. A symbol of wealth and personal power, it "honors" any gem or crystal set in it, enhancing and encouraging the action of said stone with its quickening energy. Gold also honors you. Both the softest and strongest metal, it is mutable for shaping and design, and resilient no matter how many times it is melted and reshaped. Gold never tarnishes and seems to stay beautiful and perfect through anything—it is impermeable to any weather, damage, or aging. It has been used for arthritis, and since it is impervious to harm, it is a tremendous element for renewal and regeneration. Gold has been said to help with blood and circulation, chemical and hormonal imbalances, stress-related illnesses, pulmonary problems, the brain, and also the emotional realm.

Silver moon magic

Silver is aligned with the moon and the planet Mercury, named after the quicksilver messenger god, and contains the properties associated with excellent communication. Although a healing metal, it should not be worn all the time; let your body tell you when it feels right. With this simple safeguard, you will not exhaust the power silver has to heal you. This metal offers a reflection of your self-esteem, and one should pay very special attention to this. It is a detoxifying agent that communicates with the body to alert it of raised levels of hormones and other chemical imbalances. Silver is good to wear as a necklace as it is very beneficial to the throat and lungs. Your synapses even fire more efficiently, because it acts as a transmitter. Consequently, silver is good for people encountering memory reduction problems, psychological issues, and conditions affecting your brain.

Copper contains the energy of the earth

Copper jewelry has immense healing properties and, if worn on the left side of the body, can actually prevent sickness. It is the metal most often consciously worn by healers. Because of copper's power as a conductor, healers place their faith in its ability to heal the body and mind. Copper stimulates the flow of energy throughout the body and mind, and can raise personal energy. People who suffer from lethargy should wear this metal to get out of their rut. Copper is believed to be a helpmate to the blood, soft tissue, immune system, metabolism, and mucous membranes. Long associated with positive effects on self-esteem, it gives its wearer a feeling of freedom and possibility and acts as a purifier. Copper gives confidence, and quite frankly, who could ask for anything more?

ADVANTAGEOUS ADORNMENTS

Ankle bracelets can be very healing, especially if the crystal beads are on a copper wire. Jewelry in this area of the body is also grounding and stabilizing. If you are dealing with anxiety or substance-abuse issues, wear amethyst around your ankle. If you're feeling drained of energy, jasper or rose quartz will come in handy. Rhodonite will do the trick if you are feeling disconnected or restless. Carnelian will help with circulation and calcite will strengthen your bones.

CRYSTAL CAVE CONSECRATION: MEDITATING WITH MOTHER EARTH

Even when you don't have your crystals with you, you can harness their power through powerful visualizations, such as this one. Find a quiet place where you won't be interrupted to perform the following meditation. You may wish to record it so you can listen to it with closed eyes.

Blessed beings, you are about to enter the Crystal Cave of our great Mother Earth, Gaia. In your mind, you are standing with bare feet on the ground. You can feel the grass with your toes, the solid earth underneath your feet. Feel the solidity and fastness of the earth fill your body with strength; we are all made of earth, of clay. *We come from the earth and we are made of earth.* Feel your connection to the Mother. *We come from the earth, her womb. We are made of stardust, clay, and the waters of the ocean.* Feel the blood in your veins, the water of life. Know that you are alive. Feel her winds, the breath of life. Breathe deeply ten times, completely filling your lungs and completely emptying your lungs. Breathe and feel your chest expand, rising and falling with each breath.

Now feel your backbone connecting to the earth; you feel a silver cord connecting you and your life to the earth. Concentrate on the cord until you can feel it running all the way through you and deep into the earth.

Tug on the cord; feel it give. Now, take the cord in your hands and follow it down, down, deep into the earth. It is dark as you go down and down, but you are not at all frightened, as you are a denizen of the dark. *Trust in the universe and keep descending into the bosom of the Mother.* Down we go, not falling, but moving purposefully, gracefully, following the cord into the earth. Now you can see light. Keep moving toward the light and keep holding the cord as it leads you to the shining distance.

The light grows nearer, and you see that it is an opening—a cave, a safe place for shelter. Enter the cave. It is filled with firelight reflecting off a thousand crystal points. A lovely and mysterious older woman sits near the fire, warming her bones in her comfortable and dry cave. She is bestrewn with jewels and is dressed in a velvet and gossamer robe that is iridescent and shines in the firelight. Her visage is that of an incredibly wise woman, and you can simply tell she has the knowledge of all time and the history of the world.

The cave is beautiful, more beautiful than the palace of any king or queen. It is the Crystal Cave of the Goddess, and you are with her. Show your respect to the Goddess and light the incense at her altar at the side of the cave, which has piles of many shimmering stones and priceless gems, the bounty and beauty of our generous benefactor. Sit at her feet and take in her love, power, and grace. Sit quietly and hear the special message she has for you. *You are her child, and she has dreamed a dream for you.* When you have received your Goddess-gifted message, let the cord guide you back to the surface. Release the cord and bow in gratitude to the Great Goddess.

Chapter 8

PAGAN PRAYERS FOR HEALING:
Solo and Group Intentions

In my practice, I facilitate ritual for others. I teach them how to create their own spells, lead groups, and, most importantly, fully experience rituals and be in the moment, whether flying solo or in a group rite. People who attend my workshops are surprised to learn that when they light a candle in gratitude or supplication to a higher power, they are in fact performing a ritual. Rituals may be complex and dramatic, or they may be as simple as floating a single blossom on the surface of a bowl of water. What matters is your *intention* as you perform your action. Being aware of your magical intentions and the meaning behind your practice brings a deeper significance to your actions. This all leads to greater self-understanding and it is also a way to discover the world around you. As you make your way through the enchantments herein, I encourage you to take a note from the wise healers of yore and be in tune with nature every step of the way.

BANISHING RITUAL

A friend of mine gets a cough every January like clockwork and has not quite figured out what causes it. In addition to some good common-sense practices and extra attention to hydrating, herbal teas, and healthy food with lots of rest, we performed the following banishing ritual together outdoors. You can perform this ritual with one friend or in a group.

Gather together

Outdoor table

Black tablecloth

Bowl of water

Frankincense incense and burner

Gray candle

Sharp knife

Large fireproof dish

3-foot (3-meter) length of thin jute or cotton rope

Clary sage essential oil

Together, cover the table with the tablecloth to create a simple outdoor altar. Place the water, incense, candle, knife, fireproof dish, and rope on the altar.

The person who needs to release the illness or difficulty raises their right hand, as everyone says these words aloud:

May this place this night

Be consecrated before the spirits of earth,

Air, fire, and water,

For we gather here to perform a peaceful parting

We hereby banish _____ [fill in the name of the illness or what needs to be banished].

The person releasing illness or difficulty says their name aloud, then lights the candle and incense. The same person then takes the rope and carefully cuts it in half. Place the rope pieces in the fireproof dish and let it burn completely.

Repeat the prayer and end the ritual by saying these words together:

May all be well, may I be well.

Blessings to all and blessed be.

Extinguish the candle and the incense in the water bowl. Each participant should scatter the ashes from the rope on a patch of earth nearby. Everyone should take some water and pour it on the ashes.

SPELLCASTER SMUDGING RITE

Here is a marvelous way to "reset" yourself and forge a new path for yourself with fire.

Light the sage and smudge the area well, then place it in your fire-safe vessel. Sit around the fire, relax, and think about what challenges you face and need to overcome in your life. Are there any habits you need to release from your life? Any negative self-talk? Write on a separate piece of paper each issue that comes up for you. Then, with clear intention, place each paper on the fire.

Take a moment of silent meditation, then write your hopes for the future on a new piece of paper. Fold the paper and carry it with you in your purse or wallet. Your vision for the future will take on a life of its own.

End the ritual with another sage smudging and make sure the fire is completely out before you go back inside. You should perform this rite at least once a year.

Gather together

Sage bundle

Fire-safe vessel—a fireplace, outdoor firepot, or grill

Several pieces of paper and a pen

SOLO SPIRIT WORK

While the term "vision quest" comes from Native American teachings, it is really the passage of the personal journey, no matter what your spiritual orientation is. For true personal development, it is essential to do inner work. You must explore yourself deeply and discover what is important to you, sense where you need to go, and set your spiritual goals. At the end of the day and at the end of your life, it will not matter how many houses or cars you have; what will really matter is what kind of person you were and how you treated others.

Is the work of your life soul work (spiritual development)?

Do you express yourself creatively?

Do you take care of your family? Do you help others?

Look inside; face these questions. Can you answer them satisfactorily? By doing so you will be able to determine and change the future course of events. These are the questions you'll ask yourself in your vision quest. It is an essential step in a life well lived, one that is full of soul work.

Before your quest

To ready yourself for your inner work, you should fast for one day with juice, weak tea, and plenty of water. If you have access to a sauna, you can perform a purification rite to ready your spirit. Pack a bag with a sage smudge stick, matches, water, juice, a blanket, a cell phone, and anything you feel you need for safety in case of an emergency, such as snacks and energy drinks.

Let someone know what you plan to do and where you plan to do it, and ask them to meet you at a specified time to bring you home; the last thing you'll want to do is trek to the bus or drive a car. While Native shamans traditionally sent people out into the wild, it is better to be safe. Select a garden or nearby park. Ideally, your place will be outdoors but if that is not possible, you can choose some place different to contemplate. Research the place you have selected so there are no surprises that can interfere with your plans.

Performing your vision quest

Draw a circle in the dirt, sand, or grass with a fallen branch or with your feet. Bless the circle with sage smoke and choose rocks to mark the four directions. Now settle into being alone, utterly alone. Pray, meditate, and contemplate for as long as you can without any interruptions: no food, no books, no cell phone. Pay attention to nature around you and be prepared to receive a visit from your totem animal (see below) in the form of a vision. Think about who you are and where you are going, your origins, and your spirit. Take a journal and make notes when you feel inspired. Chanting and singing is a good way to open your spirit. No two vision quests will be alike. I cannot predict what will happen to you, whether you will have epiphanies, breakthroughs, visions, or how insight will come to you. What I do know, however, is that you will undoubtedly know yourself better at the end of your vision quest.

You should always close this deeply personal rite by expressing gratitude for the place that gave you sanctuary and provided safe harbor to nature, ancestors, spirits, and energies.

Finding your animal totems

Native American tribes have given us the great gift of animal wisdom. This wonderful lore and legacy handed down to us can act as a daily oracle. When you see an animal or a representation of one, consider these meanings.

Bear: emerging consciousness

Beaver: building, manifesting hopes and dreams

Bobcat: mystery and secrets, stealth and silence

Buffalo: abundance and right livelihood

Bull: fertility

Cat: magic, the unknowable, autonomy

Coyote: wisdom, recklessness

Deer: kindness and tenderness, adventure and incorruptibility

Dog: faithful guardianship

Whale: song and music, inner intensity, creation

Wolf: ritual and spirit, allegiance and custodianship

SELF-CARE BY THE STARS

Look to the zodiacal wheel for wellness guidance given to you at birth with your natal chart. I highly recommend www.astro.com for an easy way to learn your birth chart. Find your sun sign in the list below and discover the approaches to your personal wellbeing that are excellent for you.

Aries

Arians need to sweat and work out their energy! High intensity exercise sessions with lots of cardio are key. Ideally, rams should find a workout buddy who is also a fiery type so you can compete with each other, which will make it all the more enjoyable.
Intention: I will find healthy outlets for my energy and joyful ways to share it.

Taurus

Taureans need to make sure they get high-quality sleep, which is more and more of a challenge these days. Invest in yourself by acquiring an excellent mattress that has been tested so you know it suits your sleeping style. Get proper shades to keep out the light. Try a meditation chillout sound machine and greet every new day with a bounce in your step.
Intention: I will allow myself rest and meditate for deeper peace.

Gemini

Geminis are always racing along, so can easily get ungrounded and find that they are living in their heads and keen minds all the time. This is common for all air signs and can be managed nicely through breathwork and focus. A mindful approach to breathing on a daily basis will make all the difference.
Intention: I will ground myself every day.

Cancer

Cancers can really worry and fret, leading to emotional ups and downs. Meditation can uplift you and wrest your mind away from anxieties, helping you retain a more even keel. Experiment until you find what works for you and incorporate this into both mornings and evenings, so you feel stronger in both mind and spirit.
Intention: I will leave worry behind and embrace balance in my daily life.

Leo

Leos are gutsy and like to act as if everything is going wonderfully by hiding cares and woes under a brave front. Meanwhile, their stomach might be a wreck, often upset. Ginger root tea will calm down digestive issues. Chop a couple of slices of fresh ginger, pour freshly brewed hot water over them, and drink when cooled enough. Don't let poor gut health get in the way of greatness!

Intention: I will let go of stress and embrace blessings in my life.

Virgo

Virgos are the sign of the zodiac that has the highest affinity for the healing arts. Combine that with Virgo's love of information and you will be off to a marvelous start. Creating healing mantras and setting specific meditations to incorporate regularly into your life can be an excellent practice for you that you should share and teach to others.

Intention: I will learn the healing arts to improve my wellbeing and that of my friends and loved ones.

Libra

Librans have mastery of the arts and should incorporate creativity into their wellness regimen. From doodling to drawing and painting, imaginative pursuits can be very therapeutic, as well as helping to reduce stress and engender calm. Whether painting a beautiful mural or penning a poem, the Libran virtuosity in fine arts will greatly increase your wellness quotient.

Intention: I will channel my creativity into an increasing sense of daily happiness and healthiness.

Scorpio

Scorpios are often discussed as the most intense of signs, which can be very true, but they don't get the credit deserved for their capacity for soaring spirituality and devotion to soul growth. A hot yoga practice that pushes the boundaries and gets a good sweat going can detox your body and your mind. Negative emotions, anger, grudges—let it all go out and let it all go!

Intention: I will release anything that no longer serves me and become more whole in body and soul.

Sagittarius

Sagittarians' robust health comes from their natural affinity for movement. Every Sagittarian I have hiked with gallops along, and walking as a meditation is a splendid way to exercise both body and mind in contemplation. This adventurous and philosophical sign always has a lot going on, and oftentimes, a bit too much, so a moving meditation is ideal, including walking labyrinths or going on a pilgrimage.
Intention: I will reach new heights of understanding and physical wellbeing as I explore each day in movement.

Capricorn

Capricorns are usually climbing the mountain of success, and their hard work gets Goats to the top. However, when that tips over into workaholic, you may wear yourself out. Keep an eye on that and add an element of journaling into your schedule, making time for it every day. Journaling is a kind of mindfulness so it is highly beneficial and also relaxing, which can be tough for hard-charging Capricorns. It provides a way to organize your thoughts and find out new realizations about yourself. Journal your way to joy!
Intention: I will find serenity, peace of mind, and self-compassion each day and in every way.

Aquarius

Aquarians should study crystals, gems, and stones, not only as metaphysical medicine but also for scientific understanding and making new breakthroughs on healing crystals. Thomas Edison was ostensibly one of the greatest inventors and thinkers of all times and he carried quartz crystals in his pocket and slept with them, calling them his Dream Crystals. Use these sacred stones to focus your mind and connect with emotions and higher qualities, such as kindness, love, patience, and charity. Find your magical stones and tell the world!
Intention: I will live in both my body and my mind and discover tools for self-healing.

Pisces

Pisces are renowned as the dreamers of the zodiac and are natural healers when it comes to growing healing herbs and flowers and creating potions and floral waters, as well as essential oil blends and bath salts that can be extremely innovative. Follow your famous intuition and experience and explore Mother Nature's vast array of organic curatives as you restore yourself and your loved ones with green witchery.
Intention: I will harness my psychism, enabling me to soar in the art of caring for myself and my loved ones.

GODDESS BLESS: SEEKING HELP

I recently had a great difficulty that came about quite suddenly—a negotiation on behalf of a relative with an international corporation that involved a potential loss of a business and a large amount of money. Nothing I tried was working. At one point, things became so fraught that I turned to the ancestors for help and asked very specifically for what was needed. I remember tearing up during the ritual because of the pressure and stress of it all. Within one hour, my prayers and requests were heard and resolved. The guardians will be there for you, too.

Calling upon guides and helpers for aid is easy. Simply say:

Guardians from the light, please come to me and assist me with my _____ [fill in the blank]

You may choose to know them and can add:

Show yourselves to me; let me know your presence.

Sometimes a friend or loved one who has passed away will come, sometimes an old pet will appear, and sometimes you may feel a touch on your shoulder or a loving presence. Trust these moments. You can always ask, "Who is with me from the light?" If you feel a strange presence that makes you uncomfortable, ask who it is or simply ask the energy to go to the light and leave your space now.

Calling on angels
When you feel the need for help from your angel guides and your higher self, you can call on them, too. They are always present, but to actively work with you they must be invited. I call them like this:

Angels, Archangels, please come and be with me now. I would like your presence with me for this healing. Higher Self, please work with me now.

I also call all my guides and animal allies (see page 133) every time that I create my sacred space.

SPELL TO HONOR THE SUPERNATURAL

You can call upon any god or goddess with whom you feel a deep connection, but I advise you take some time to explore. You might be surprised what you discover as there are many deities—some are listed opposite. An unknown god or goddess might help you reveal unseen and unknown sides of yourself.

Decide what will be a suitable offering to the deity of your choice. If it is a sea spirit, perhaps a beautiful seashell. If it is an earth goddess, a gorgeous crystal would be just right.

Place an offering to your chosen divinity on your altar or shrine—perhaps a verse of poetry or a painting or drawing—that shows your gratitude and appreciation for all you have received and will continue to receive as inspiration. Chant aloud:

O _____ [name of deity], wise and true,

I will walk with thee in the fields of paradise and back.

Anoint me here and now.

Thanks to you, _____ [repeat name of deity], I will never lack.

In gratitude and service, blessed be thee.

GREAT GODS AND GODDESSES

There are many deities you can call upon; here are just a few that can particularly help support your wellbeing. Call on them for rituals, and look for signs and symbols connected to them in your everyday life—they are watching over you.

Ceres

Ceres is the great Roman grain goddess. Think of her every time you have some cereal, which is named after her. The early summer festival, the Cerealia, honors Ceres for supplying the harvest and an abundance of crops. Any ceremony for planting, growing, and cooking could involve this bounty-bringer. If you are going to plant a magical garden, craft a ritual with Ceres and make an outdoor altar to this grain goddess.

Adonis

Adonis does not get nearly enough credit as a god of healing. He is better known as the legendary god of love, and partner of the goddess of love, Aphrodite. Adonis is also an herbal deity with domain over certain plants and flowers, representing earth, fertility, and health. He is often invoked for love rites and spells. Ask Adonis for help with your gardens and for healing.

Osiris

Osiris is the Egyptian god of death and rebirth who also takes care of the crops, the mind, the afterlife, and manners. Husband to Isis and father of Horus, Osiris is a green god who is deeply connected to the cycles of growing and changing seasons. Turn to this god for rites of remembrance and for help with grief and mourning.

Sunna

Sunna is the ancient Germanic goddess of the sun, making clear that the big star in the nearby sky has not always been deified as male. The Teutons also referred to this very important divine entity as the "Glory of Elves." In the great poetic epic, the Eddas, it was said she bore a new daughter Suhn, who sheds light on a brand-new world. Other sun goddesses include the Arabic Atthar, the Celtic Sulis, and the Japanese Amaterasu. As you rise each morning, speak your greeting to Sunna. Morning rituals set a positive tone for the day, ensuring that you are indeed living a magical life.

Aganippe

Aganippe's abode was on Mount Helicon in ancient Greece, in a wellspring that was sacred to the muses. Living in these sacred waters gave Aganippe the ability to confer inspiration upon poets; inspiration flowed as well in the water drunk from the rivers and brooks that had their source in her spring. She is the daughter of the river deity Ternessus. An especially charming part of this myth is that the wellspring was created by the hooves of Pegasus.

The Eye Goddess

The Eye Goddess is an extremely ancient Mediterranean deity. She was a goddess of justice in the form of a pair of huge, unblinking eyes, and no transgression could be concealed from her. The Eye Goddess's first appearance was around 3,500 BCE. You can conjure the Eye Goddess's powers of justice with the depiction of eyes and invoke her assistance any time you need the truth brought to light. You can also practice simple protection magic for the home and for your car with eyes watching out for you. Her symbol is sometimes mistaken for the evil eye, which makes workers of mischief nervous and causes thieves to think twice before committing a crime.

Juno

Juno watches over the daughters of the earth, and as such attends nearly every female need and function. The Latin word for a female soul is *juno*, and as the mother of all women she can be invoked in any woman's mystery of birth, menses, croning, and death. Some of her aspects include a goddess of fate, Juno Fortuna; of war, Juno Martialis; of marriage, Juno Domiduca; of bones, Juno Ossipaga; of mother's milk, Juno Rumina. Because Juno is a special protector of brides, you can invent a Juno-centered ceremony to celebrate your own nuptials or those of a friend who espouses women's spirituality.

CONCLUSION: FINDING YOUR SOUL-CARE STRATEGIES

I am very grateful to everyone who has helped bring about the era of self-care in which we live; it was well-timed, and I am sure it is also here to stay. I believe this will only increase and I have also been very pleased to see other folks delve into the old ways and bring back folk healing from many wisdom traditions. The hedgewitches and medicine men and women of centuries past were rooted in the wisdom of the natural world through practice and study, and made sure to pass down the hard-won knowledge to the next generation. To a great extent, that is what we have here, where I have adapted those healing spells, rites, and practices for modern times.

There is a simple and profound reason to take the time for tending your own wellbeing and care of the soul: it will greatly add to your joy quotient. It might take time for you to notice, but if you delve into daily rituals and self-care spells, you will very gradually and steadily become lighter and brighter. One day, you'll wake up and realize that you feel really good.

Now and again, I make tweaks to my routine—including new teas and tincture recipes, alternative approaches to herbs and foods, and different essential oils and balms. Recently, I felt the need to change it up even more with many of the enchantments and witchy wellness ideas herein. Dear reader, I am thrilled to tell you that I feel better than I have in years. In addition to the practices and ritual remedies, I have incorporated a great consciousness about my health, both physical and spiritual. It is a kind of mindfulness that you can easily add to your days by setting your personal healing intention (see page 10) and holding that positive energy. It is one of the best things you can do for yourself and will enrich your sense of wellbeing from this day forward. Blessed be!

Index

Acknowledgments

Deep thanks to the duo of Kristine Pidkameny and Carmel Edmonds who are marvelous editors and as creative and inspiring as any heavenly muse. The exceptionally lovely illustrations, thanks to the work of Emma Garner, add their magic and make the book a work of art, brought together by Geoff Borin's design. Publisher Cindy Richards and her team are contributing some of the most beautiful books being published today—so much so that I have a little shrine with my books by CICO on it, along with a few other sacred objects. When I hold one of my treasured books in my hand, I can literally feel the love, care, and great attention paid to every detail. And for that, I am grateful. Brava!